SpringerBriefs in Computer Science

For further volumes:
http://www.springer.com/series/10028

Ricard Prados · Rafael Garcia
László Neumann

Image Blending Techniques and their Application in Underwater Mosaicing

Ricard Prados
Rafael Garcia
László Neumann
University of Girona
Girona
Spain

ISSN 2191-5768   ISSN 2191-5776   (electronic)
ISBN 978-3-319-05557-2   ISBN 978-3-319-05558-9   (eBook)
DOI 10.1007/978-3-319-05558-9
Springer Cham Heidelberg New York Dordrecht London

Library of Congress Control Number: 2014934137

Printed on acid-free paper

Springer is part of Springer Science+Business Media (www.springer.com)

To my mother, R. P.
To Àlex, Laia and Yolanda, R. G.
To my father, L. N.

Preface

Underwater surveys have numerous scientific applications in the fields of archeology, geology, and biology, involving tasks such as ancient shipwreck prospection, ecological studies, environmental damage assessment, and detection of temporal changes. When diving at extreme depths or during long periods of time, underwater surveys are nowadays carried out by Underwater Vehicles (UV). These vehicles are often equipped with advanced navigation sensors, including optical cameras. Optical imaging provides short-range, high-resolution visual information about the ocean floor.

Scientists can benefit from these images as they provide, from the cognitive point of view, the most precise and accurate representation of the areas surveyed, enabling a detailed analysis of the structures of interest. The underwater medium adds particular challenges to the image acquisition task, and phenomena such as light attenuation enforce it to be performed as close to the seabed as possible. Hence, optically mapping large seafloor areas can only be achieved by building image mosaics from a set of reduced-area pictures, *i.e., photo-mosaics*. Unfortunately, the seams along image boundaries are often noticeable, due to photometrical and geometrical registration inaccuracies. *Image blending* is the merging step in which those artifacts are minimized. Processing bottlenecks and the lack of medium specific processing tools have restricted underwater photo-mosaics to small areas despite the hundreds of thousands of m^2 that modern surveys can cover. Large underwater photo-mosaics are in increasing demand for the characterization of the seafloor for scientific purposes. Producing these mosaics is difficult due to the challenging nature of the underwater environment and of the image acquisition conditions, including extreme depth, scattering and light attenuation phenomena, and difficulties in vehicle navigation and positioning.

This book proposes strategies and solutions to tackle the problem of building photo-mosaics of very large underwater optical surveys, *i.e. Giga-mosaics*, presenting contributions in the image preprocessing, enhancing, and blending steps, and resulting in an improved visual quality of the final photo-mosaic.

First, a comprehensive review of the current and most prominent state-of-the-art mosaicing and blending techniques is provided in Chap. 3, in order to evaluate their application in the underwater imaging context. A classification criterion for the existing methods is presented, based on their main features and performance.

Second, a full approach for large-scale underwater image mosaicing and blending is proposed. In the image preprocessing step, a depth-dependent illumination compensation function is used to solve the nonuniform illumination appearance due to light attenuation. Additionally, if depth information is not available, a depth estimation based on the size of the image projection (once registered) is exploited in different steps of the pipeline. Concerning image enhancement, the image contrast variability due to different acquisition altitudes is compensated using an adaptive contrast enhancement based on an image quality reference selected through a Total Variation (TV) criterion. This criterion is also applied to give a higher priority to the information coming from higher quality images, making the contribution from sharper and more informative images higher than that of contrastless or poorly detailed ones. In the blending step, a graph-cut strategy operating in the image gradient domain over the overlapping regions is proposed. This approach allows finding an adequate seam even if the overlapping images have been acquired with different exposures. A smooth transition around the optimally selected seams is performed in a narrow strip, ensuring the maximum possible sharpness and avoiding double contouring problems. Finally, an out-of-core blending strategy for very large-scale photo-mosaics is presented and tested on real data, generating images surpassing the giga-pixel order, and having, as its only limitation, the maximum size of the tile that can be processed in the computer's memory.

The performance of the proposed approach and the benefits of using blended gigamosaics for interpretation tasks are evaluated in Chap. 5. The results obtained by the proposed method are discussed and compared with other state-of-the-art approaches, using a series of challenging large-scale underwater datasets.

Contents

Acronyms

AUV	Autonomous Underwater Vehicle
BA	Bundle Adjustment
BCM	Brightness Constancy Model
CLAHE	Contrast Limited Adaptive Histogram Equalization
DOF	Degree Of Freedom
DVL	Doppler Velocity Log
EKF	Extended Kalman Filter
GA	Global Alignment
GDIM	Generalized Dynamic Image Model
GPS	Global Positioning System
HDR	High Dynamic Range
HOG	Histogram of Gradients
LBL	Long Baseline
LMedS	Least Median of Squares
MEX	Matlab EXecutable
MST	Minimum Spanning Tree
RANSAC	Random Sample Consensus
ROD	Region of Difference
ROV	Remotely Operated Vehicle
SEF	Seam-Eliminating Function
SIFT	Scale Invariant Feature Transform
SNR	Signal-to-Noise Ratio
SSD	Sum of Squared Differences
SURF	Speeded Up Robust Features
TV	Total Variation
USBL	Ultra Short Baseline
UV	Underwater Vehicle

Chapter 1
Introduction

Abstract This chapter introduces the reader to the problem of high-quality large-scale underwater optical mapping, as well as to the need for blending techniques to improve the quality of the generated maps. Underwater surveys are nowadays carried out by Underwater Vehicles (UVs), which allow diving at extreme depths during long periods of time. Optical imaging provides short-range high-resolution visual information of the ocean floor. Unfortunately, several medium-specific phenomena, such as light attenuation and scattering, constrain the acquisition by limiting the maximum area covered by a single image. Hence, optically mapping large seafloor areas can only be achieved by building image mosaics from a set of reduced area pictures, i.e. photo-mosaics. Blending techniques provide a set of heterogeneously appearing images of a given map with a continuous and consistent appearance. Beyond visual appearance, blending techniques are also important for proper interpretation and scientific exploitation of seafloor imagery. Finally, the book structure is outlined at the end of the chapter.

Keywords Underwater mapping · Photo-mosaicing · Blending techniques · Light attenuation · Scattering

1.1 Background

Seafloor exploration is an ancient activity that started thousands of years ago with human shallow diving [1]. Nowadays, underwater surveys have numerous scientific applications in the fields of archeology [2], geology [3, 4] and biology [5], involving tasks such as ancient shipwreck prospection [6], ecological studies [7, 8], environmental damage assessment [9, 10] or detection of temporal changes [11], just to name a few.

Due to human limitations when diving at extreme depths or during long periods of time, underwater surveys are nowadays carried out by UVs. UVs can be either

R. Prados et al., *Image Blending Techniques and their Application in Underwater Mosaicing*, SpringerBriefs in Computer Science, DOI: 10.1007/978-3-319-05558-9_1,
© The Author(s) 2014

Fig. 1.1 Illustration of an underwater vehicle acquiring images at low altitude due to the constraints imposed by the medium. Poor lighting conditions require the use of artificial lighting, which in addition to light attenuation leads to non-uniform lighting and induced shadows in the acquired images. Scattering and moving objects, such as fish or algae are some of the other specific challenges that appear due to the particularities of the acquisition medium

Autonomous Underwater Vehicles (AUVs) or Remotely Operated Vehicles (ROVs), which are manually controlled by a pilot. These vehicles are often equipped with advanced navigation sensors. Typical sensor suites may include an Ultra Short Base Line (USBL), a Long Base Line (LBL), a Doppler Velocity Log (DVL), accelerometers, inclinometers, acoustic imaging sensors and optical cameras, among others, depending on the type, size and cost of the vehicle.

Among the sensors listed above, optical imaging provides short-range high-resolution visual information of the ocean floor. In the scientific scope, archeologists, geologists and biologists can benefit from these images as they provide the most precise and accurate representation of the areas surveyed, from the cognitive point of view, enabling a detailed analysis of the structures of interest.

Nevertheless, the underwater medium adds particular challenges to the image acquisition task (see Fig. 1.1). When an underwater vehicle acquires images in deep waters, light attenuation has a huge impact on the visibility range and color reproduction, especially when the vehicle navigates at changing altitude (i.e. distance from the camera to the seafloor). Due to the light attenuation phenomenon, image acquisition needs to be performed close to the seabed, considerably limiting the maximum area covered by a single photograph. Hence, optically mapping large seafloor areas can only be achieved by building image mosaics from a set of reduced-area pictures.

The history of large-scale, deep-sea optical mapping starts with the French-American Mid-Ocean Undersea Study (FAMOUS) project [12], in 1974. In this survey, the Alvin submersible explored the great rift valley of the Mid-Atlantic Ridge, southwest of the Azores. The cruise was planned based on large sequences of images supplied by the US Navy, which were manually aligned on a gymnasium floor, i.e. a *photo-mosaic*.

Over the last decade, the relevance of photo-mosaicing has grown significantly. As a clear example, numerous off-the-shelf still cameras now include built-in algorithms to fuse several pictures from a panoramic sequence into a single wide-angle view. Furthermore, gigapixel photo-mosaics [13] of the entire Earth are easily available through the Internet, using a limited bandwidth connection. In most cases, such large mosaics are created from terrestrial, aerial or space related imagery. The common photo-mosaicing problems for this kind of image, comprehending the compensation of different exposures and non-uniform illumination, have been treated in the literature [14–20].

Unfortunately, performing underwater image surveys is a challenging task with a much higher level of complexity than conventional terrestrial or aerial image photo-mosaic generation. As stated in [21], and due to constrained image acquisition conditions, both the navigation data and the images acquired have to be used to recover an accurate estimate of the camera poses during the survey. This information fusion is often performed by means of Global Alignment (GA) techniques [21–24]. This is a mandatory step before generating precise visual maps of the seafloor. In most cases, the short distance between the camera and the seafloor produces *parallax* effects (see Fig. 1.2), which considerably affect 2D mosaicing approaches due to the violation of the planarity assumption, i.e. the assumption of a flat scene, which allows the computation of 2D transformations between images. Furthermore, suspended particles causing the *scattering* phenomenon [25] are commonly present. Moving elements, such as fish and algae, are examples of other common issues in underwater image processing.

Using the navigation data collected by the UV allows us to estimate the camera poses during the acquisition. Consequently, from these camera poses the vehicle trajectory can also be recovered. Once an initial guess of this trajectory is obtained, it can be refined through global alignment techniques by using the information from the acquired images. As a result of this processing pipeline, the acquired images can be projected and rendered into a single and common reference frame. Nevertheless, it is necessary to perform one last step to give the heterogeneously appearing image dataset a continuous and uniform appearance in the form of a single large mosaic. This is achieved by means of *image blending* techniques (see Fig. 1.3).

Apart from the visual appearance, blending techniques are also important for proper interpretation and scientific exploitation of seafloor imagery (e.g. [26, 27]). The structures and objects of interest may cover a wide range of scales, from a few centimeters, i.e. macrofauna or rocks which would appear in individual images, to several tens or hundreds of meters, i.e. topographic scarps or fractures spanning thousands of images. To correctly analyze such varying features, and to understand the spatial relationships that may exist (e.g. faunal assemblages associated with geological features), it is preferable to have a single, wide area photo-mosaic, in which imaging artifacts are minimized, and identified features of interest may be accurately represented regardless of their size and imaging conditions.

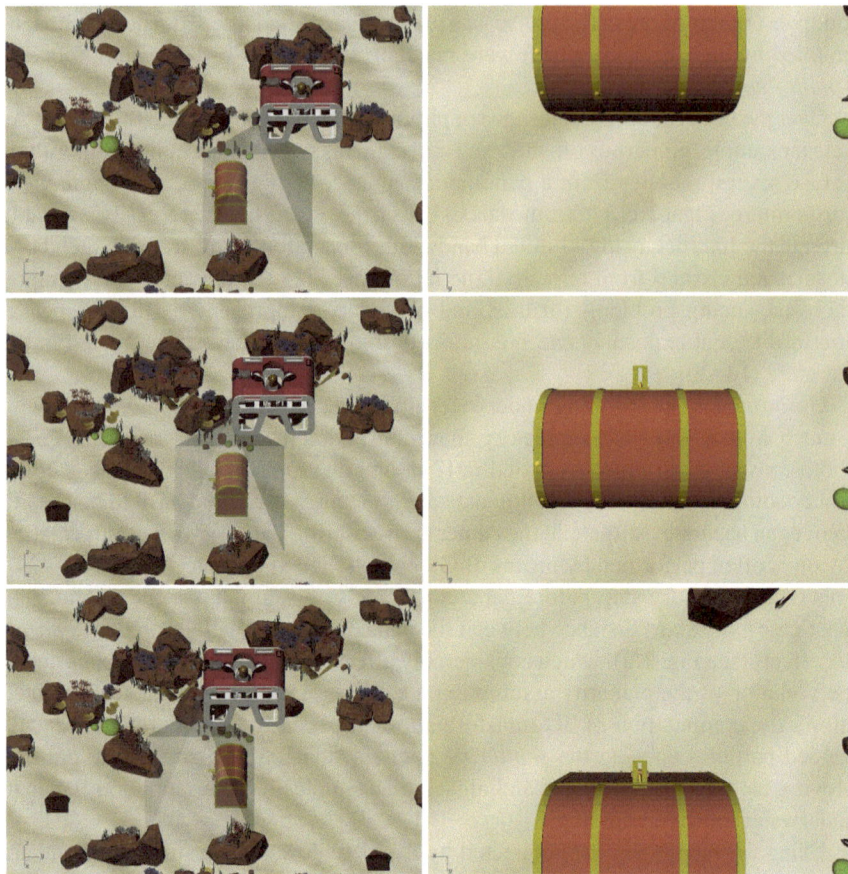

Fig. 1.2 Sequence corresponding to a straight trajectory of an AUV depicting the parallax problems. It shows the side and camera views of the robot's trajectory. One side of the chest disappears from the frame while the other arises due to the parallax effect

1.2 Challenges of Underwater Optical Imaging

According to John F. Brown [28], the first underwater picture (Fig. 1.4) was taken by William Thompson in February 1856 in Dorset (England). The photographer lowered a housed 5" × 4" plate camera to the seabed in Weymouth Bay and operated the shutter from an anchored boat. The exposure time used to acquire the picture was 10 min during which time the camera flooded, however the film was salvaged. Scuba diving, which can be intuitively considered as a more conventional way to acquire underwater images, did not exist as a common activity until several years later.

Acquiring optical images underwater is significantly more difficult than performing conventional land photography. Submerging a camera underwater using an adequate housing and maneuvering it appropriately is a complex task by itself. However,

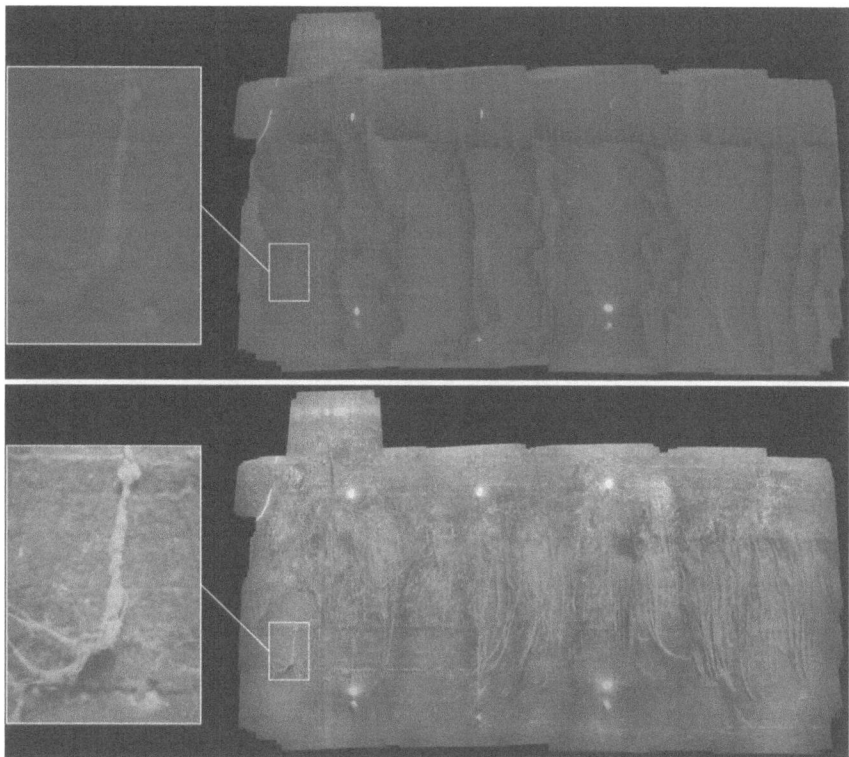

Fig. 1.3 Underwater mosaic of a dam and zoomed detail before (*top*) and after (*bottom*) the application of an image blending technique. In the blended mosaic, the elements on the dam wall (mainly algae) are clearly visible, whereas in the non-blended mosaic they are hardly distinguishable

the most important challenges are imposed by the underwater medium properties affected by several phenomena which condition the acquisition procedure. The two main underwater phenomena strongly affecting image quality and consequently the acquisition task are *light attenuation* and *scattering* [19].

Apart from these two main phenomena, the camera parametrization is another key point affecting image quality. When acquiring images underwater using a still camera, the automatic adjustment mechanism may try to slow the shutter speed and increase the aperture in order to better deal with the low light conditions. This setup is very sensitive to camera movement and thus, unsuitable for a camera mounted on an AUV or ROV. When the acquisition is performed in shallow waters, the ambient light can be sufficient to acquire quality images, but when performed in deep waters high power artificial light sources are required. Using artificial light, typically consisting of one or more directional sources, leads to another problem affecting images, especially when registering them to build a mosaic, which is non-uniform illumination of the scene. Finally, when using artificial lighting, the shadows induced

Fig. 1.4 The first underwater
image in history taken
by William Thompson in
February 1856 in Dorset
(England) with an
almost totally submerged
photographic camera (*source*
Christian Petron, History of
Underwater Image, Digital
Edition, 2011)

on the scene create an apparent motion which is opposite to the real motion of the
camera.

Light Attenuation

Sunlight wavelengths in the visible spectrum for a typical human eye range from
390 nm (violet tones) to 770 nm (reddish tones) [29]. Light attenuation is due to
the light absorption by water, which increases exponentially with depth and affects
all wavelengths to varying degrees, and depends on the different water bodies [30].
Therefore, sun light cannot penetrate to any great depth and artificial lighting systems
are required when acquiring images several meters below the surface (see Fig. 1.6).
When using artificial light sources, such as continuous lights or strobes, the acquired
images show brighter and richer detail information in the region on which these
lights are focused, while rendering a darker and contrastless appearance of the sur-
roundings (Fig. 1.5-bottom-right). This effect is accentuated due to the *vignetting*
caused by the camera optics. Light attenuation also leads to color loss (Fig. 1.5-
bottom-left). The longer wavelengths corresponding to the reddish tones are the first
to be attenuated, while the shortest ones corresponding to the bluish tones are the
last. This loss is the reason for the greenish or bluish appearance of objects in underwater scenes as the distance between object and camera increases. Some organic
particles, such as phytoplankton frequently found in coastal waters, absorb light pre-
dominantly in the shortest wavelengths (corresponding to the blue and violet tones),
allowing only the greenish tones to persist. In order to deal with light attenuation in
seafloor mapping, high power and appropriately distributed artificial light sources
should be used, and image acquisition should be performed as close to the seabed as
possible.

Fig. 1.5 (*Top-left*) Example of *backward scattering* due to the reflection of rays from the light source on particles in suspension, hindering the identification of the seafloor texture. (*Top-right*) Example of *forward scattering* caused by the local inter-reflection of light on the suspended particles, hiding the terrain behind them. (*Bottom-left*) Image depicting the effects of *light absorption* in the underwater medium, where longer wavelengths are first absorbed, causing the bluish appearance of the scene structures at a lower depth. (*Bottom-right*) Effects produced by *light attenuation* of the water resulting in an evident loss of luminance in the regions farthest from the focus of the artificial lighting

Scattering

The presence of organic and inorganic particles suspended in the volume of water intersected by the field of view of the camera and the illumination source (see "scattering volume" in Fig. 1.7) is the cause of the light scattering phenomenon. This is illustrated in Fig. 1.5-top. It can be strongly noticeable when caused by a suspended sediment load (also known as turbidity). The degree of scattering depends on the distance, the wavelength, and the characteristics of the particles (i.e. shape, density

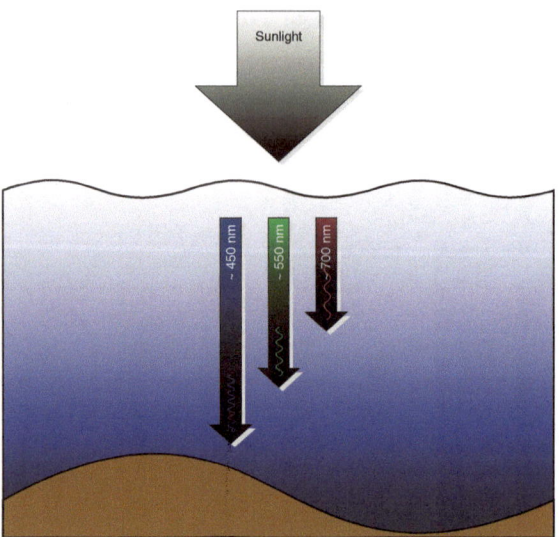

Fig. 1.6 Light attenuation in the visible spectrum range (from 390 nm to 770 nm) prevents sun light wavelengths from reaching long distances below the water surface. The longer wavelengths corresponding to the reddish tones are the first to be attenuated, while the shortest ones corresponding to the bluish tones are the last

and refractive index). There are two types of scattering. On the one hand, *backward scattering* is an additive noise in the form of "marine snow" patterns which appear due to the reflection of the light from a given natural or artificial source on the suspended particles in the direction of the camera. On the other hand, *forward scattering* appears due to the inter-reflections of local light among the particles, and becomes the most significant source of image degradation leading to a non-uniform loss of contrast, definition and color fidelity. The scattering phenomenon can significantly affect the acquisition of images at a short distance from seabed. The vehicle carrying the camera may also cause the displacement of particles or soil lying on the ground, increasing the probability of *backward scattering*.

1.3 Objectives

The numerous scientific applications of underwater optical imaging require providing experts with the most informative and visually pleasant representations possible of the seafloor. Underwater surveys carried out by both AUVs or ROVs generate a large volume of navigation and optical imaging data. This information needs to be post-processed and managed in such a way that makes its study by the scientists

Fig. 1.7 The scattering effect appears in the volume of water intersected by the field of view of the camera and the illumination source

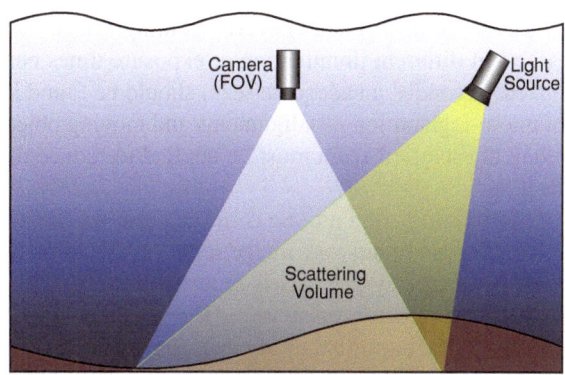

(e.g. [26]) as easy as possible or even just feasible. In that sense, photo-mosaics are an adequate way to manage, unify and consistently fuse all this optical imaging data and unite it with the navigation data to generate georeferenced maps. Providing the maps generated with a convincing and reliable appearance has not only aesthetic but cognitive purposes. The interpretation of a given scene becomes more intuitive and effective when its representation emphasizes its features and has a global smooth and continuous overall appearance.

Building a photo-mosaic from a large set of underwater images is a challenging task. The quality of every single picture might change considerably along the sequence due to the underwater lighting phenomena described above. Furthermore, the computational requirements to process this large amount of data from a given imaging survey limit the maximum size of the map generated.

Consequently, the goal of this book is to propose a complete blending approach using state-of-the-art methods capable of generating and blending large scale optical maps. The blending technique developed is focused on two main ideas. Firstly, the richness of detail in the original images should not only be preserved but also enhanced when possible. Secondly, the algorithms should be able to deal with datasets of thousands of images covering large areas of the seafloor (to the order of several hundreds of thousands of m^2). Consequently, the processing strategy needs to deal with underwater imaging while being well-suited for large input sequences.

1.4 Outline of the Approach

A single, large image, i.e. a photo-mosaic, is easier to interpret than a long sequence of consecutive pictures or even a video record, inasmuch as it offers a spatially and photometrically consistent representation of the seabed. In order to ensure this image consistency, blending techniques are required. These techniques, which produce a seamless mosaic, enable the interpretation of the benthos by a scientist (biologist, geologist, archeologist, etc.).

There are three main concerns guiding image blending algorithms. Firstly, the effects of different illumination or exposure times between images should be minimized. Secondly, an adequate seam should be found in order to reduce the visibility of micro-registration misalignments and moving objects. Lastly, a smooth transition along the selected seam must be applied to reduce the visibility of seams between images.

The topology of a mosaic is initially estimated based on the navigation data and a feature-based pair-wise image registration. After this initial estimation, a global alignment strategy [21, 22] is required to reduce the cumulative error of a simple sequential pair-wise registration. The strength of the global alignment arises from closing-loops, because they allow us to significantly improve the camera's trajectory estimate when re-visiting an already mapped area. In the absence of loop-closings, and considering input sequences of thousands of images, the drift accumulated by the pair-wise transformations leads to significantly inconsistent (missaligned) photo-mosaics.

Aside from *exposure variations*, which are a common issue in terrestrial images, the remaining problems are not directly addressed by conventional panorama generation software. To better deal with the inherent underwater imaging problems (*non-uniform illumination, light attenuation, scattering, exposure variations*, etc.), we perform image pre-processing, which, in our experience, is a key step, strongly impacting the quality of the final photo-mosaic rendering. A depth adaptive inhomogeneous lighting compensation algorithm is proposed to deal with the non-uniform distribution of the artificial light sources in the scene whose effects are emphasized due to the *light attenuation* phenomenon. Concerning image detail enhancement, a gradient based image enhancement depending on the distance from the camera to the seabed, has also been proposed. Both *scattering* and *light absorption* phenomena may lead to highly variable appearances for images depicting the same area but acquired at significantly different depths. The aim of this enhancement is to bring the closest appearance to the involved images in order to achieve a consistent fusion.

Once the images have been preprocessed, thus making them more suitable for an adequate blending, an image selection algorithm based on image quality is applied, with two main aims. Firstly, to reduce the number of images to be processed with the next step algorithm and consequently reduce the computational cost. Secondly, to avoid lower quality images negatively affecting the appearance of the regions also covered by higher quality ones.

Next, a hybrid luminance-gradient graph-cut based optimal seam finding algorithm is proposed to locate the seams which minimize the photometric and morphological differences in the image boundaries. The proposed algorithm is able to robustly deal with differently exposed images, thanks to the gradient term, especially when image preprocessing is not enough to palliate these differences.

Then, we apply a gradient blending strategy in a narrow region around the optimally computed seams in order to ensure a smooth transition between the image patches involved. Additionally, the gradient nature of the blending also allows us to compensate eventual exposure differences between images.

Finally, a gigamosaic generation strategy is presented, based on the decomposition of the large-dimension mosaics into tiles of reasonable size that can be processed in conventional computers without large amounts of resources.

1.5 Contributions

The main contributions of this book can be summarized as follows:

- A novel full mosaicing and blending pipeline optimized for underwater imaging is proposed. The effects of underwater phenomena such as non-uniform illumination and scattering are compensated for in an adaptive way, with the main aim of not only preserving, but also emphasizing, image detail richness.
- An adaptive image enhancement algorithm has been developed to make fine image details sharper, also providing a continuous and consistent appearance to the whole mosaic image. The enhancement of a given image is determined by the detail richness of the adjacent images, but avoids overemphasizing the result.
- The optimal seam finding algorithm used to determine the most adequate path for the cut between images is based on both luminance and gradient information. This domain combination allows us to ensure not only the lowest photometric differences along the path but also to avoid cutting objects, even in the case of significant exposure differences between images.
- In order to address the problem of processing large datasets, a strategy allowing us to independently process different regions of the final mosaic is proposed. The area corresponding to a large dimension mosaic is divided into a regular grid of tiles, which are then individually processed, temporarily stored and finally fused to obtain the final single image. The appearance consistency between individual tiles is ensured thanks to an exposure equalization mechanism.
- The full processing pipeline has been devised to use parallel processing in every step where possible in order to improve the overall performance of the approach.

1.6 Book Structure

The book is divided into the following chapters:

Chapter 2 presents an introduction to a feature-based 2D mosaicing framework. The main concepts of planar motion estimation and global alignment are introduced.

Chapter 3 reviews the state of the art in image blending techniques, presenting the two main principles guiding the algorithms. A classification of techniques is also proposed, based on their main features. The benefits and drawbacks of the different methods are discussed, as well as their suitability for underwater imaging purposes.

Chapter 4 details the proposed processing pipeline optimized for high resolution
              underwater image blending. All the steps involved, including original
              image preprocessing, image registration and global alignment, selection
              of image contribution, optimal seam finding strategy and gradient domain
              image blending, are described. Finally, a giga-mosaic blending strategy
              is presented.

Chapter 5 shows some experimental high-resolution results, based on large datasets,
              which are also discussed and compared to results obtained by other state-
              of-the-art approaches.

Chapter 6 presents the conclusions of this work, summarizes the contributions and
              identifies some future research directions.

References

1. Somers, L.H.: History of diving: Selected events, Aug 2002
2. Eustice, R., Singh, H., Leonard, J.J., Walter, M.R.: Visually mapping the rms titanic: conserv-
    ative covariance estimates for slam information filters. Int. J. Robot. Res. **25**(12), 1223–1242
    (2006)
3. Zhu, Z., Riseman, E., Hanson, A., Schultz, H.: An efficient method for geo-referenced video
    mosaicing for environmental monitoring. Mach. Vis. Appl. **16**, 203–216 (2005). doi:10.1007/
    s00138-005-0173-x
4. Escartin, J., Garcia, R., Delaunoy, O., Ferrer, J., Gracias, N., Elibol, A., Cufi, X., Neumann,
    L., Fornari, D.J., Humphris, S.E., Renard, J.: Globally aligned photomosaic of the lucky strike
    hydrothermal vent field (Mid-Atlantic ridge, 37° 18.5'N): release of georeferenced data, mosaic
    construction, and viewing software. Geochem. Geophys. Geosyst. **9**(12), 12(1)–12(17) (2008).
    ISSN: 1525-2027. doi:10.1029/2008GC002204
5. Pizarro, O., Singh, H.: Toward large-area mosaicing for underwater scientific applications.
    IEEE J. Oceanic Eng. **28**(4), 651–672 (2003)
6. Drap, P., Scaradozzi, D., Gambogi, P., Gauch, F.: Underwater photogrammetry for archaeology-
    the venus project framework. In: GRAPP, pp. 485–491 (2008)
7. Jerosch, K., Lüdtke, A., Schlüter, M., Ioannidis, G.T.: Automatic content-based analysis of
    georeferenced image data: detection of beggiatoa mats in seafloor video mosaics from the
    hakon mosby mud volcano. Comput. Geosci. **33**(2), 202–218 (2007)
8. Lirman, D., Gracias, N., Gintert, B., Gleason, A., Reid, R., Negahdaripour, S., Kramer, P.:
    Development and application of a video-mosaic survey technology to document the status of
    coral reef communities. Environ. Monit. Assess. **125**, 59–73 (2007). doi:10.1007/s10661-006-
    9239-0
9. Gleason, A.C.R., Lirman, D., Williams, D., Gracias, N., Gintert, B.E., Madjidi, H., Pamela,
    R., Chris, B.G., Negahdaripour, S., Miller, M., Kramer, P.: Documenting hurricane impacts on
    coral reefs using two-dimensional video-mosaic technology. Mar. Ecol. **28**(2), 254–258 (2007)
10. Lirman, D., Gracias, N., Gintert, B., Gleason, A., Deangelo, G., Dick, M., Martinez, E., Reid,
    R.P.: Damage and recovery assessment of vessel grounding injuries on coral reef habitats using
    georeferenced landscape video mosaics. Limnol. Oceanogr. Methods **8**, 88–97 (2010)
11. Delaunoy, O., Gracias, N., Garcia, R.: Towards detecting changes in underwater image
    sequences. In: Proceedings of the MTS/IEEE OCEANS Conference. Kobe, Japan, pp. 1–8
    (2008)
12. Heirtzler, J.R.: Project famous. Rev. Geophys. **13**(3), 542–542 (1975)
13. Kopf, J., Uyttendaele, M., Deussen, O., Cohen, M.: Capturing and viewing gigapixel images.
    ACM Trans. Graph. (SIGGRAPH) **26**(3), 93(1)–93(10) (2007)

14. Uyttendaele, M., Eden, A., Szeliski, R.: Eliminating ghosting and exposure artifacts in image mosaics. In: Proceedings of the International Conference on Computer Vision and Pattern Recognition (CVPR), pp. 509–516 (2001)

15. Jia, J., Tang, C.-K.: Image registration with global and local luminance alignment. In: Proceedings of the IEEE International Conference on Computer Vision (ICCV), vol. 1, pp. 156–163, Oct 2003

16. Litvinov, A., Schechner, Y.Y.: Radiometric framework for image mosaicking. J. Opt. Soc. Am. **22**(5), 839–848 (2005)

17. Zhao, W.: Flexible image blending for image mosaicing with reduced artifacts. Int. J. Pattern Recogn. Artif. Intell. **20**(4), 609–628 (2006)

18. Cheng, Y., Xue, D., Li, Y.: A fast mosaic approach for remote sensing images. In: International Conference on Mechatronics and Automation (ICMA), pp. 2009–2013, Aug 2007

19. Garcia, R., Nicosevici, T., Cufi, X.: On the way to solve lighting problems in underwater imaging. In: Proceedings of the MTS/IEEE OCEANS Conference, vol. 2, pp. 1018–1024, Oct 2002

20. Rzhanov, Y., Gu, F.: Enhancement of underwater videomosaics for post-processing. In: Proceedings of the MTS/IEEE OCEANS Conference, pp. 1–6, Oct 2007

21. Ferrer, J., Elibol, A., Delaunoy, O., Gracias, N., Garcia, R.: Large-area photo-mosaics using global alignment and navigation data. In: Proceedings of the IEEE OCEANS Conference, pp. 1–9, Oct 2007

22. Elibol, A., Garcia, R., Delaunoy, O., Gracias, N.: A new global alignment method for feature based image mosaicing. In: Proceedings of the International Symposium on Advances in Visual Computing (ISVC), Part II. SpringerVerlag, Berlin, Heidelberg, pp. 257–266 (2008)

23. Elibol, A., Gracias, N., Garcia, R.: Augmented state-extended kalman filter combined framework for topology estimation in large-area underwater mapping. J. Field Robot. **27**(5), 656–674 (2010)

24. Elibol, A., Garcia, R., Gracias, N.: A new global alignment approach for underwater optical mapping. Ocean Eng. **38**(10), 1207–1219 (2011)

25. Shao, B., Jaffe, J.S., Chachisvilis, M., Esener, S.C.: Angular resolved light scattering for discriminating among marine picoplankton: modeling and experimental measurements. Opt. Express **14**(25), 12473–12484 (2006)

26. Barreyre, T., Escartin, J., Garcia, R., Cannat, M., Mittelstaedt, E., Prados, R.: Structure, temporal evolution, and heat flux estimates from a deep-sea hydrothermal field derived from seafloor image mosaics. Geochem. Geophys. Geosyst. **13**(4), 1–29 (2012)

27. Mittelstaedt, E., Escartin, J., Gracias, N., Olive, J.A., Barreyre, T., Davaille, A., Cannat, M., Garcia, R.: Quantifying diffuse and discrete venting at the Tour Eiffel vent site, lucky strike hydrothermal field. Geochem. Geophys. Geosyst. **13**(4), 1–18 (2012). ISSN: 1525-2027. doi:10.1029/2011GC003991

28. Brown, J.F.: Br. J. Photogr. (1985)

29. Starr, C., Evers, C.A., Starr, L.: Biology: Concepts and Applications. Brooks/Cole, Belmont (2010)

30. Wozniak, B., Dera, J.: Light Absorption in Sea Water. Atmospheric and Oceanographic Sciences Library, vol. 33. Springer, New York (2007)

Chapter 2
Underwater 2D Mosaicing

Abstract The current chapter describes the main steps involved in the photo-mosaic building process. These steps comprehend the geometrical registration and warping of the images into a single common reference frame, along with an estimation of the topology of the trajectory performed by the UV, and a global alignment of the recovered trajectory. A widely extended geometrical registration strategy consists of identifying common image features between the involved images, using different image feature detectors. These image features, once identified, become correspondences that are used to estimate the camera motion between consecutive images, as well as to perform a global alignment of the estimated trajectory. Global alignment of all the involved images allows providing geometrical consistence to the underwater map. At the end of the chapter the problems and issues of the photo-mosaicing process are pointed out, with the aim of demonstrating the relevance of image blending techniques as a final step of the photo-mosaicing process.

Keywords Photo-mosaicing · Image registration · Image alignment · Image warping · Topology estimation · Global alignment · Deep-ocean surveys

Building a photo-mosaic is a task involving two main steps. Firstly, the images should be geometrically registered and warped accordingly into a single common reference frame. Secondly, the rendering of the mosaic should be performed through blending techniques, which allow us to deal with photometric differences and reduce the visibility of registration inaccuracies between the images involved (see Fig. 2.1).

In the context of large-scale underwater photo-mosaicing, deep-ocean surveys are typically composed of hundreds to hundreds of thousands of images. These images are affected by several underwater phenomena, such as the aforementioned scattering and light attenuation, and the sequences may present small or even nonexistent overlaps between consecutive frames. For these reasons, navigation data coming from acoustic positioning sensors (USBL, LBL), velocity sensors (DVL), inclinometers or gyroscopes might be used to estimate the trajectory of the vehicle. This trajectory can

R. Prados et al., *Image Blending Techniques and their Application in Underwater Mosaicing*, SpringerBriefs in Computer Science, DOI: 10.1007/978-3-319-05558-9_2, © The Author(s) 2014

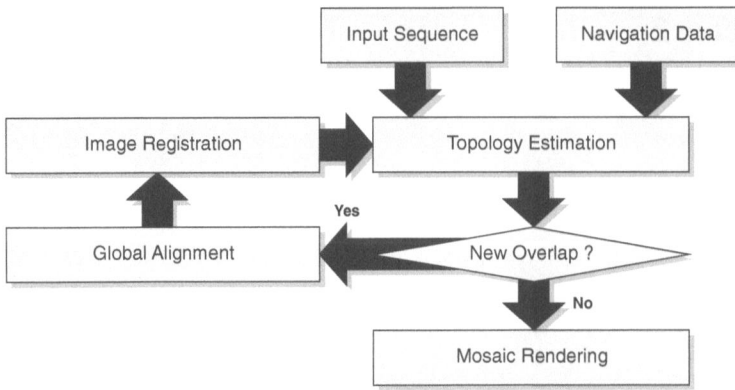

Fig. 2.1 Underwater mosaicing pipeline scheme. The *Topology Estimation, Image Registration,* and *Global Alignment* steps can be performed iteratively until no new overlapping images are detected

be later refined by computing *pair-wise alignment* and applying a *global alignment* method [1–7].

2.1 Topology Estimation

When lacking sensor positioning data, such as USBL, LBL or DVL, using time-consecutive image registration, assumed to have an overlapping area, may become the only strategy to estimate the trajectory of the robot and, thus, the motion of the camera. This dead-reckoning estimate suffers from a rapid accumulation of registration errors, leading to drifts from the actual trajectory, but it does provide useful information for non-time-consecutive overlapping images. Matching non-time-consecutive images is a key step in refining the trajectory followed by the robot using global alignment methods. With the refined trajectory, new-non time-consecutive overlapping images can be predicted and attempted to match. This iterative matching and optimization process continues until no new overlapping images are detected. The procedure described is known as *topology estimation* [8, 9] (see Fig. 2.2). If navigation data is available, the topology estimation remains as an indispensable step to obtain globally consistent mosaics and accurate trajectory estimates, specially when dealing with sequences of a large number of images.

Deep-ocean surveys composed of thousands of images make any kind of all-to-all image pair matching strategy to perform a topology estimation unfeasible. Therefore, more sophisticated approaches are needed to perform this task. Elibol et al. [8] proposed an Extended Kalman Filter (EKF) framework, aimed at minimizing the total number of matching attempts and simultaneously obtaining the best possible trajectory. Potential image pairs are predicted by taking into account

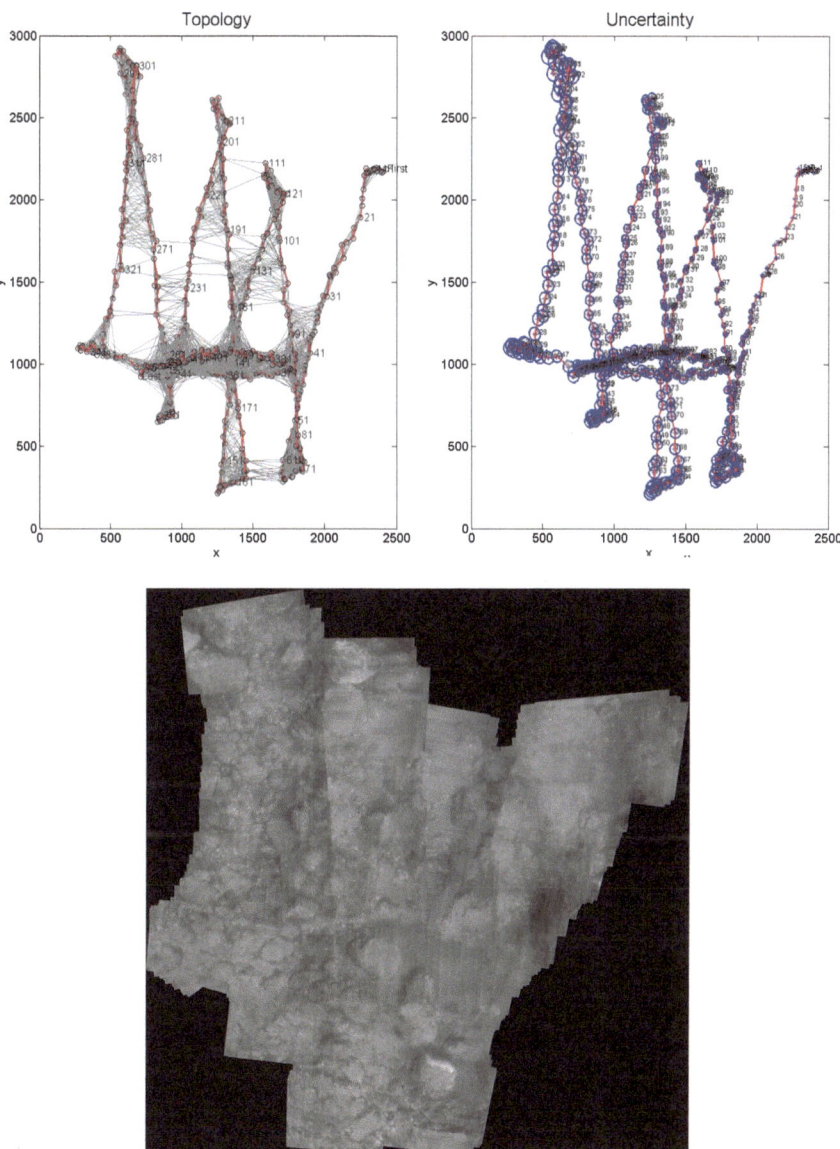

Fig. 2.2 Topology estimation scheme. (*Top-left*) Final trajectory obtained by the scheme proposed in [8]. The first image frame is chosen as a global frame and all images are then translated in order to have positive values in the axes. The x and y axes are in pixels and the scale is approximately 150 pixels per metre. The plot is expressed in pixels instead of metres since the uncertainty of the sensor used to determine the scale (an acoustic altimeter) is not known. The *red lines* join the time-consecutive images while the *black* ones connect non time-consecutive overlapping image pairs. The total number of overlapping pairs is 5,412. (*Top-right*) Uncertainty in the final trajectory. Uncertainty of the image centres is computed from the covariance matrix of the trajectory [5]. The uncertainty ellipses are drawn with a 95 % confidence level. (*Bottom*) Mosaic built from the estimated trajectory

Fig. 2.3 Geometric registration of two different views of the same underwater scene by means of a planar transformation

the uncertainty of the trajectory. Additionally, a different solution to the topology estimation problem in a Bundle Adjustment (BA) framework was proposed in [10]. To obtain a tentative topology, a fast image similarity criterion combined with a Minimum Spanning Tree (MST) solution are used. The topology is improved by attempting image-matching with the pairs of images for which there is the most overlapping evidence.

2.2 Image Registration

Aligning in 2D two or more images taken from different viewpoints consists of finding an appropriate planar transformation which allows overlaying them into a single and common reference frame (see Fig. 2.3). This step, essential in the image mosaicing pipeline, is known as the image registration problem [11] and has been greatly discussed in the literature [12, 13].

The geometrical registration can be performed by means of *direct methods* or *feature-based methods*. Sections 2.2.1 and 2.2.2 present these two main groups of image registration methods.

2.2.1 Direct Methods

This first group of algorithms, also known as feature-less methods, compute the transformation between images by maximizing the photometric consistency over the whole overlapping image regions, and are found to be useful for large overlapping regions as well as small translations and rotations [12, 14, 15]. These methods can be classified in turn into *frequency domain based methods* and *optical flow methods*.

Frequency Domain

Methods based on the frequency domain originally used phase-correlation to estimate the shifts (translations) between an image pair. Later, extensions to account for rotation and scale transformations [16] and affine transformations [17] using log-polar coordinates were also proposed. In practice, the number of authors proposing the use of frequency domain methods for underwater image registration is small [18, 19]. This group of methods are computationally expensive, as they require Fast Fourier Transform (FFT) to be computed over all the images involved.

Optical Flow

Optical flow methods are based on the estimation of the disparity (i.e. apparent motion) of pixels between image pairs. Generally, the optical flow estimates the flow field using the Brightness Constancy Model (BCM), in which it is assumed that the photometric properties of image pixels (luminance and color) remain constant. There are two main groups of algorithms estimating the optical flow. On the one hand, *global methods* such as Horn and Schunck [14] yield dense flow fields, while, on the other hand, *local methods* such as Lucas and Kanade [20, 21] produce non-dense regularized grid flow fields but are less robust to noise. Over the last years, some authors have proposed more robust alternatives to BCM that assume linear changes in illumination, using the Generalized Dynamic Image Model (GDIM) [22, 23] and the color information [24, 25]. Due to the formulation of the problem, optical flow methods are not suited for disparities that exceed 1 pixel. To overcome this issue, multi-resolution approaches such as [26] have been proposed. In this case, the images are gradually decimated and the optical flow is computed from coarse levels towards fine levels. Unfortunately, the method also has some drawbacks. Firstly, it is slow because the optical flow has to be computed at each level. Secondly, the maximum pixel disparity has to be known *a priori* in order to set the number of decimation levels. Furthermore, multi-resolution approaches are very sensitive to noise, since errors in the estimation of optical flow at coarse levels propagate to the fine levels.

2.2.2 Feature-Based Methods

The second group of methods rely on the computation of a transformation between images using a sparse set of points [27–31] and correspondences. Contrarily to direct methods, feature based methods do not require a high frame-rate to ensure a high percentage of overlap between consecutive images. For these reasons, feature-based methods are the most widely used in the literature to perform image registration, and are also used in the work presented, as described in the following sections.

There are two main strategies concerning feature-based pair-wise image alignment (see Fig. 2.4). The first strategy consists of locating the interest points in one image of

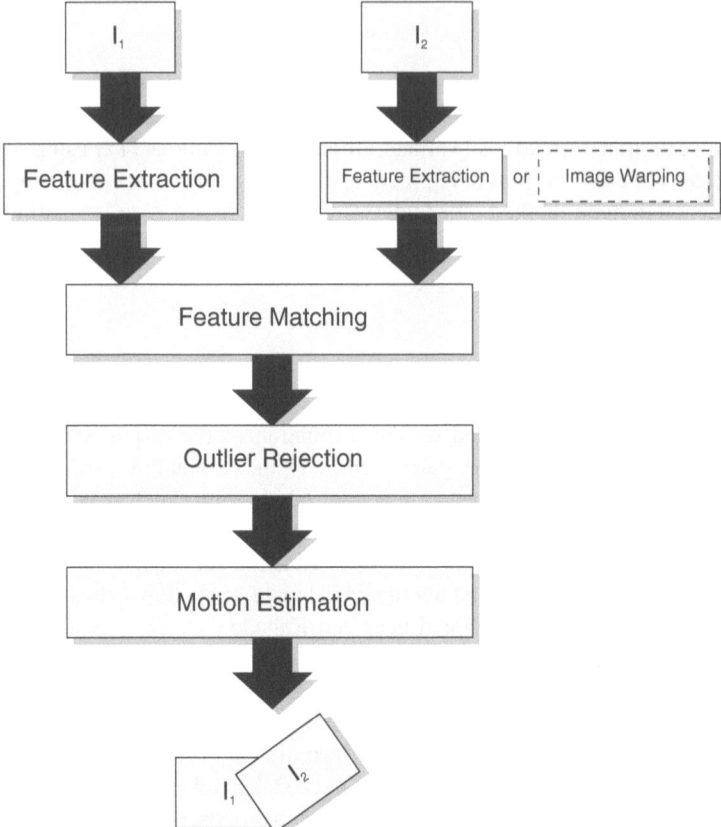

Fig. 2.4 Main steps involved in the pair-wise registration process. The Feature Extraction step can be performed in both images of the pair, or only in one. In this last case, the features are identified in the second image after an optional Image Warping based on a transformation estimation

the pair using some feature detector, such as Harris and Stephens [27], Beaudet [28] or Lindeberg [29], and identifying these in the other. The correspondence problem is solved using cross-correlation or a Sum of Squared Differences (SSD) measure, which is computed using the information of the pixels surrounding the feature, and compared to the value of this measure for a given window of pixels in the other image. The procedure has the advantage of obtaining highly accurate correspondences when changes in rotation and scale are moderate. As a drawback, this strategy requires some prior knowledge to determine the estimated translation between images and the size of the search window, in addition to not being suitable for large changes in rotation and scale. For these reasons, this approach might be used as a refinement step of certain feature-based image alignment strategies [5], after an appropriate warping of the image in which the features found should be identified.

The second strategy is based on the detection of features in both images using invariant feature descriptors, such as SIFT [30], its faster variant SURF [31] (which uses an approximation of the Laplacian and Hessian detectors respectively) or others, and performing the matching, comparing their descriptor vectors. The SIFT descriptor is based on Histograms of Gradient (HOGs) computed in the area surrounding the detected interest points, while SURF describes a distribution of Haar wavelet [32] responses within the neighborhood of the interest point. These feature detectors and descriptors are known to show invariance to a wider range of geometrical and photometrical [33] transformations of the images than the detectors mentioned above. Therefore, these detector and descriptor properties allow us to obtain very robust results, even in the case of strong rotations or scale changes between frames and significant illumination inhomogeneities.

2.3 Motion Estimation

2.3.1 Planar Homography

The planar transformation between two different views of the same flat scene can be described by means of a *planar homography* matrix [34, 35]. This homography is able to describe a motion with up to eight Degrees of Freedom (DOF).

Let us consider a point p, belonging to a 2D plane Π in 3D space. Then, the projections of p into two different images I_1 and I_2 are given in $x_1, x_2 \in \mathbb{R}^3$ in homogeneous coordinates. Also let the coordinate transformation between the two frames be

$$\mathbf{X}_2 = R\mathbf{X}_1 + T \tag{2.1}$$

where $\mathbf{X}_1, \mathbf{X}_2 \in \mathbb{R}^3$ are the 3D coordinates of p relative to camera frames 1 and 2, respectively, taken at times t_1 and t_2. The two projections x_1, x_2 of p in images I_1 and I_2 satisfy the epipolar constraint [34]

$$x_2^T E x_1 = x_2^T \widehat{T} R x_1 = 0 \tag{2.2}$$

where E is the essential matrix, containing information about the relative position T and orientation R between the two camera frames 1 and 2, and $\widehat{T}$ is the skew-symmetric matrix codifying position T [35].

However, for points on the same plane Π, their images will share an extra constraint that makes the epipolar constraint alone no longer sufficient.

Let $N = [n_1, n_2, n_3]^T \in \mathbb{S}^2$ be the unit normal vector of the plane Π with respect to the first camera frame, and let $d > 0$ denote the distance from the plane Π to the optical center of the first camera. Then we have

$$N^T \mathbf{X}_1 = n_1 X + n_2 Y + n_3 Z = d \quad \Leftrightarrow \quad \frac{1}{d} N^T \mathbf{X}_1 = 1, \quad \nabla \mathbf{X}_1 \in \Pi \qquad (2.3)$$

Substituting Eq. (2.3) into Eq. (2.2) gives

$$\mathbf{X}_2 = R\mathbf{X}_1 + T = R\mathbf{X}_1 + T \frac{1}{d} N^T \mathbf{X}_1 = \left(R + \frac{1}{d} T N^T \right) \mathbf{X}_1 \qquad (2.4)$$

Then matrix H is defined as follows

$$H = R + \frac{1}{d} T N^T \in \mathbb{R}^{3 \times 3} \qquad (2.5)$$

where H is the *(planar) homography matrix*, since it denotes a linear transformation from $\mathbf{X}_1 \in \mathbb{R}^3$ to $\mathbf{X}_2 \in \mathbb{R}^3$ as

$$\mathbf{X}_2 = H\mathbf{X}_1 \qquad (2.6)$$

Note that the matrix H depends on the motion parameters R, T as well as the structure parameters N, d of the plane Π. Due to the inherent scale ambiguity in the term $\frac{1}{d} T$ in Eq. (2.5), one can at most recover from H the ratio of the translation T scaled by the distance d.

From

$$\lambda_1 \boldsymbol{x}_1 = \mathbf{X}_1, \quad \lambda_2 \boldsymbol{x}_2 = \mathbf{X}_2, \quad \lambda_2 \boldsymbol{x}_2 = H\mathbf{X}_1 \qquad (2.7)$$

we have

$$\lambda_2 \boldsymbol{x}_2 = H \lambda_1 \boldsymbol{x}_1 \quad \Leftrightarrow \quad \boldsymbol{x}_2 \sim H \boldsymbol{x}_1 \qquad (2.8)$$

where we recall that $\sim$ indicates equality up to a scale factor. Often, the equation

$$\boldsymbol{x}_2 \sim H \boldsymbol{x}_1 \qquad (2.9)$$

itself is referred to as a *(planar) homography* mapping induced by a plane Π.

The homography matrix H encodes information about the camera motion and the scene structure, a fact that facilitates establishing correspondence between points in the first and second images. H can be computed in general from a small number of corresponding image pairs.

2.3.2 Planarity Assumption

The homography matrix allows the description of 2D transformations between images. This motion estimation assumes that the scene is planar (i.e. flat), but this scenario is rare in practice. Nevertheless, it is possible to apply a homography matrix to register different views of the same scene, even if it is not planar, under certain conditions.

On the one hand, it is possible to use a homography matrix to model the transformation between images when the camera only describes a rotation or change in scale around the same optical center. On the other hand, it can also be assumed that a scene is planar when the camera describes a translation but the magnitude of the scene relief is negligible compared to the distance between the camera and the scene. In any other cases images show the *parallax* effect, i.e. the difference in the apparent position of an object viewed along two different lines of sight, measured by the angle of inclination between those two lines.

The parallax effect impacts both the registration and blending steps. When registering a pair of images showing parallax, the computed homography will try to encode the dominant motion between both views. In that case, if the structures causing the parallax are large enough with respect to the image size, errors in the motion estimation may arise. Furthermore, if two images suffering from parallax are successfully registered, i.e. the dominant motion has been correctly estimated, evident misalignments may appear when overlying both views. This scenario is common in underwater imagery, where the distance between the camera and the scene is not always as important as desired, and consequently image blending techniques have to deal with this problem.

2.3.3 Outlier Rejection

The homography accuracy [36] is strongly tied to the quality of the correspondences used for its calculation. The homography estimation algorithms assume that the only source of error is the measurement of the locations of the points, but this assumption is not always true inasmuch as mismatched points may also be present. There are several factors that can influence the goodness of the correspondences detected. Images can suffer from several artifacts, such as non-uniform illumination, sun flickering (in shallow waters), shadows (specially in the presence of artificial lighting) and digital noise, among others, which can make matching fail. Furthermore, moving objects (including shadows) may induce correspondences which, despite being correct, do not obey the dominant motion between the two images. These correspondences are known as *outliers*. Consequently, it is necessary to use an algorithm able to discern right and wrong correspondences. There are two main strategies to reject outliers widely used in the bibliography [37]: Random Sample Consensus (RANSAC) [38] and Least Median of Squares (LMedS) [39]. LMedS efficiency is very low in presence of Gaussian noise [40, 41]. For this reason, RANSAC has been selected as outlier rejection method in the presented framework.

RANSAC is a robust estimator intended to fit a model to experimental data and is able to smooth data containing a significant percentage of gross errors. This feature makes the approach suitable for image processing applications, where error-prone data is quite frequent. As stated in [38], contrary to other smoothing techniques, instead of using as much data as possible to obtain an initial solution and then attempting to eliminate the invalid data, RANSAC uses a small set of data as a point of departure and enlarges this set with consistent data when possible. When there is enough data, RANSAC can use a smoothing technique, such as least squares, to compute an improved estimate for the parameters of the model with the mutually consistent data which has been identified. The RANSAC paradigm is tuned up by three parameters: the error tolerance used to determine the compatibility of a given data point to the model, the number N of subsets S_i with size s used to instantiate the model and the threshold T that determines the number of points required to consider that a correct model has been found. RANSAC tries to compute a model candidate based on a set of s data points from S selected randomly. The model is next applied to the rest of the data in order to determine the set of points S_i that are within a distance of a defined threshold. If the size of S_i is greater than any predefined threshold T, the model can be re-estimated with the points in S_i. Otherwise, if the size of S_i is lower than T, a new subset is selected and the process is repeated. After N trials, the largest consensus set S_i is selected and the model is re-estimated. Reliable RANSAC estimates requires that at least one of the candidate models contains the correct parameter values, otherwise the estimator loses its effectiveness.

2.4 Global Alignment

Pair-wise registration of images acquired by an underwater vehicle equipped with a down-looking camera cannot be used as an accurate trajectory estimation strategy. Image noise, illumination issues and the violation of the planar assumption may unavoidably lead to an accumulative drift. Therefore, detecting correspondences between non-consecutive frames becomes an important step in order to close a loop and use this information to correct the estimated trajectory.

The homography matrix $^1\mathbf{H}_k$ represents the transformation ot the kth image with respect to the global frame (assuming the 1st frame frame as a global frame) and is known as *absolute homography*. This $^1\mathbf{H}_k$ matrix is obtained as a result of the concatenation of the *relative homographies* $^{k-1}\mathbf{H}_k$ between the kth and ^{k-1}kth images of a given time-consecutive sequence. As mentioned above, relative homographies have limited accuracy and computing absolute homographies by cascading them results in cumulative error. This drift will cause, in the case of long sequences, the presence of misalignments between neighboring images belonging to different transects (see Fig. 2.5).

The main benefit of *global alignment* techniques is the use of the closing-loop information to correct the pair-wise trajectory estimation by reducing the accumulated drift.

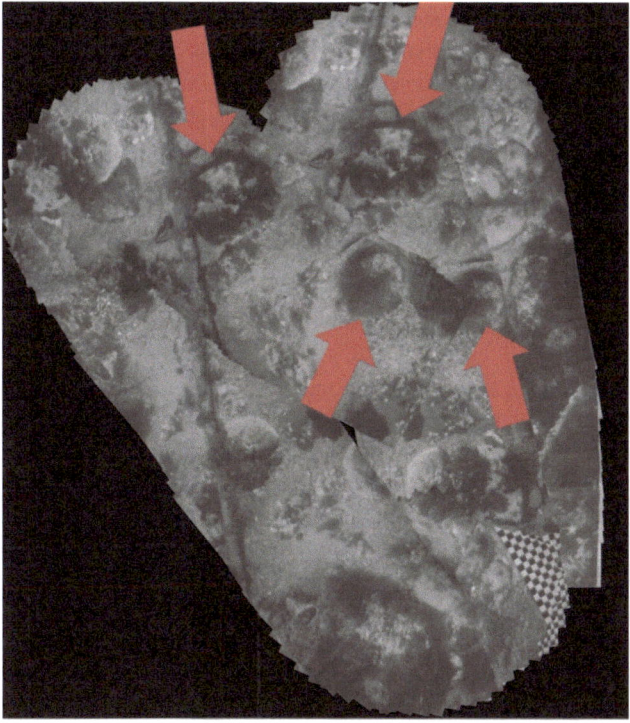

Fig. 2.5 Example of error accumulation from registration of sequential images. The same benthic structures appear in different locations of the mosaic due to error accumulation (trajectory drift)

2.4.1 Global Alignment Methods

There are several methods in the literature intended to solve the global alignment problem [42]. Global alignment methods usually require the minimization of an error term based on the location of the image correspondences. These methods can be classified according to the domain where this error is defined, leading to two main groups: image frame methods [1, 5, 43, 44] and mosaic frame methods [2, 4, 45–48].

Concerning the group of image frame based methods, Davis [45] faced the problem of a camera rotating around its optical axis without translation. The absolute homography was obtained as an accumulation of relative homographies (see Eq. 2.10), and computed solving a sparse linear systems of equations.

$$^1\mathbf{H}_i = \prod_{j=2}^{i} {}^{j-1}\mathbf{H}_j \quad i \geq 2 \tag{2.10}$$

Any image i of a given sequence can be projected to another image space j or to the global frame using the absolute homography of image j, i.e. $^1\mathbf{H}_i = {}^1\mathbf{H}_j \cdot {}^j\mathbf{H}_i$, where $^1\mathbf{H}_i$ and $^1\mathbf{H}_j$ are unknown and $^j\mathbf{H}_i$ is a relative homography. When a closing loop happens, the number of relative homographies becomes greater than the number of images, leading to an over-determined system. Unfortunately, the over parameterization of the system might lead to overfitting if an adequate parametrization of the resolution method is not used.

Another image frame based method was proposed by Shum and Szeliski [49], who defined the error function as:

$$\min_{^1\mathbf{H}_2,^1\mathbf{H}_3,\ldots,^1\mathbf{H}_N} \sum_k \sum_m \sum_{j=1}^n \| ^k\boldsymbol{x}_j - {^1}\mathbf{H}_k^{-1} \cdot {^1}\mathbf{H}_m \cdot {^m}\boldsymbol{x}_j \|_2 \tag{2.11}$$

where $^k\boldsymbol{x}_j$ and $^m\boldsymbol{x}_j$ are the jth correspondence between images k and m having an overlap area, n the number of correspondences and $\|\cdot\|_2$ the Euclidean norm. Calculating the solution by means of a non-linear least squares minimization has a drawback: the gradients with respect to the motion parameters are quite complicated and have to be provided for the minimization method chosen, e.g. Levenberg-Marquadt.

In the group of mosaic frame based methods, Sawhney et al. [2], proposed a method based on the following error function:

$$E_1 = \min_{^1\mathbf{H}_2,^1\mathbf{H}_3,\ldots,^1\mathbf{H}_N} \sum_k \sum_m \sum_{j=1}^n \| ^1\mathbf{H}_k \cdot {^k}\boldsymbol{x}_j - {^1}\mathbf{H}_m \cdot {^m}\boldsymbol{x}_j \|_2 \tag{2.12}$$

Nevertheless, this solution suffers from what is known as scaling effect of a mosaic-based cost function if no constraints are imposed. This is due to the fact that the cost function has lower values when the image size is smaller, and consequently the function tends to reduce this image size. For that reason, Sawhney et al. [2] extended the method by introducing another term for controlling the scaling effects:

$$E_2 = \sum_{i=1}^N \left(\| ^1\mathbf{H}_i \cdot \boldsymbol{x}_{tr} - {^1}\mathbf{H}_i \cdot \boldsymbol{x}_{bl} - (\boldsymbol{x}_{tr} - \boldsymbol{x}_{bl}) \|_2 + \| ^1\mathbf{H}_i \cdot \boldsymbol{x}_{tl} - {^1}\mathbf{H}_i \cdot \boldsymbol{x}_{br} - (\boldsymbol{x}_{tl} - \boldsymbol{x}_{br}) \|_2 \right)$$
$$\tag{2.13}$$

where x_{tr}, x_{bl}, x_{tl} and x_{br} denote the top-right, bottom-left, top-left and bottom-right coordinates of the image corners. E_2 tries to minimize the difference in the diagonal length between the original image size and the image size once projected on the mosaic frame. Nevertheless, this constraint may lead to image misalignments because it violates the distance minimization between correspondences. A weighting factor for this penalization is used, which can be fixed or proportionally grow along the sequence due to error accumulation. The final error function E is the result of the addition of both E_1 and E_2 terms, i.e. $E = E_1 + E_2$. The minimization of this function leads to solutions related by a common translation and rotation that have the same minima [50]. Therefore, Sawhney et al. [2] proposed a new term $\mathbf{H}_1 \cdot (0, 0, 1)^T$ to be added to the error function, in order to fix the problem with the translation of the first image and find only a single solution set. Another solution for this issue has been proposed by Gracias et al. [4], who fixed one of the image frames as the global mosaic frame and aligned all the images with respect to this one.

Sawhney et al. [2] proposed a graph-based representation of the mosaic for closed loop trajectories. In this case, each node of the graph represents an image whilst each edge represents overlapping areas between the images. Initially, the graph is built only with edges between consecutive images. Edges between non-consecutive images can be added by measuring the distances between the image centers. The goal of this graph is to reduce the total number of products by searching for the optimal path while computing absolute homographies through relative homographies [44, 46], with the aim of reducing the accumulated drift and image distortions.

In the graph representation context, Kang et al. [46] presented an approach to solve the global alignment problem also based on graphs to define the temporal and spatial connectivity between images. Initially, a regular grid of the global frame is defined. Each node of the graph contains a list of corresponding grid points and several lists with the correspondences between these grid points and the points in other images. The correspondences are computed by means of normalized correlation, and the error function is defined as the photometric luminance differences between the points in the mosaic and their projection in other images:

$$E = \sum_i (I_m(\mathbf{p}) - I_i(\mathbf{p}'))^2 \tag{2.14}$$

where $I_m(\mathbf{p})$ is the luminance value of $\mathbf{p}$ in the mosaic and $I_i(\mathbf{p}')$ is the luminance of the projection $\mathbf{p}' = {}^m\mathbf{H}_i \cdot {}^1\mathbf{p}$ in the ith image. This error function is used to find all the correspondences of each point in the initial grid. The global registration of the different frames is performed by searching for the optimal path connecting each frame to the reference frame. This path, in its turn, is computed by the geometric distance and correlation score between each grid point and its correspondences. Once the images have been registered to the global frame, the location of grid points is adjusted using as a weighting average factor the correlation score between correspondences. Finally, the absolute homographies computed from the accumulation of the relative ones can be recomputed by means of an adjustment transformation, using a linear transformation between the refined grid points and their correspondences.

Marzotto et al. [44] presented a solution close to their of Sawhney et al. [2], which adds another measure to the overlap measure in:

$$d_{ij} = \frac{\max(|x_i - x_j| - |\mathbf{r}_i - \mathbf{r}_j|/2)}{\min(\mathbf{r}_i, \mathbf{r}_j)} \tag{2.15}$$

where x_i and x_j are warped image centers and r_i and r_j are warped image diameters. This additional measure is defined as:

$$\beta_{ij} = \frac{\delta_{ij}}{\Delta_{ij}} \tag{2.16}$$

where δ_{ij} is the overlap measure and Δ_{ij} is the cost of the shortest path between nodes i and j. The optimal path is found by using β values, and the cost is calculated from the weights, d, on the edges. The absolute homographies are obtained as a result of the product of relative homographies through the optimal path. The main advantage of this method to compute the optimal path is that the homographies are less affected by cumulative errors. Similarly to [2], the error function used in the global alignment is defined over a set of grid points, being the error of a given grid point x_k:

$$E_k = \frac{1}{n} \sum_i \sum_j \| x_k - {}^m\mathbf{H}_i \cdot {}^i\mathbf{H}_j \cdot \mathbf{H}_j^{-1} x_k \|_2 \tag{2.17}$$

where n is the number of edges between images containing the grid point x_k and ${}^m\mathbf{H}_i$ and ${}^m\mathbf{H}_j$ denote absolute homographies. The error function is defined as:

$$\min E = \sum_i^m E_i^2 \tag{2.18}$$

where m is the total number of grid points. Unfortunately, there are two main drawbacks to this approach. The first is that point locations have to be carefully selected to ensure enough grid points in both images and overlapping regions in order to compute the homography. The second is that arbitrarily distributed points may fall into textureless areas, making the location of matchings difficult.

With the aim of minimizing both the homography elements and the position of features in the mosaic, Capel [3] proposed a method based on the tracking of features, which requires identifying the same feature in all the different views. Lets consider ${}^t x_i$ as the coordinates of a given i^{th} point defined in the coordinate system of image t and the projection of point ${}^m x_j$ in the mosaic, which is called the pre-image point and is usually projected in different views. All image points corresponding to the projection of the same pre-image point are called N-view matches. This approach proposes the following cost function to be minimized:

$$\varepsilon_1 = \sum_{j=1}^{M} \sum_{{}^t x_i \in \eta_j} \| {}^t x_i - {}^t\mathbf{H}_m \cdot {}^m x_j \|_2 \tag{2.19}$$

where M is the total number of pre-image points, n_j is the set of N-view matches and ${}^t\mathbf{H}_m$ is mosaic-to-image homography. Knowing that the homographies and the pre-image points are unknowns, the total number of unknowns can be be obtained as $n = n_{DOF} \times n_{view} + 2 \times n_{points}$, where n_{DOF} are the number of Degree Of Freedoms (DOFs) of the homography, n_{views} is the total number of views and n_{points} is the total number of pre-image points. The fact of measuring the error term ε_1 in the image frame but being parameterized with points defined in the mosaic frame, allows us to avoid image an scaling bias that appears when measured in the mosaic frame. As a drawback, the number of unknowns increases significantly as the size of the dataset grows, making it unsuitable for datasets with thousands of images.

BA is a technique to solve the problem of refining visual reconstruction to produce jointly optimal 3D structure and viewing parameter estimates (camera pose and/or calibration) [51, 52]. The solution is intended to be optimal with respect to both structure and camera variations. BA minimizes the reprojection error between the image correspondences. This minimization is defined as the sum of squares of a large number of nonlinear, real-valued functions, and is achieved using nonlinear least squares methods. Concerning image mosaicing, the target of BA is to find optimal camera motion parameters in order to compute absolute homographies [53]. Gracias et al. [54] presented an approach based on the minimization of the following cost function:

$$E = \sum_{i,j} \sum_{k=1}^{n} \left(\|^i x_k - ^i \mathbf{H}_j \cdot^j x_k\|_2 + \|^j x_k - ^i \mathbf{H}_j^{-1} \cdot^i x_k\|_2 \right) \qquad (2.20)$$

where n is the number of matches between images i and j. The total number of unknowns is $6 \times (n_{views} - 1) + 2$. The method requires knowing the intrinsic camera parameters and has high computational requirements due to the use of nonlinear optimization algorithms.

For further details of advantages and disadvantages of the different GA methods the reader is addressed to [55].

2.5 Conclusions

Building photo-mosaics of underwater image surveys is a complex task that faces medium-specific challenges not present in terrestrial or aerial panorama generation. Due to the lack of natural light in deep waters, the UVs should integrate artificial lighting systems. The power of the light sources is limited, specially due to autonomy reasons, and typically does not allow uniform illumination of the whole area covered by a picture. The effects of this lack of power are accentuated by the underwater phenomenon of light attenuation, which leads to a noticeable non-uniform illumination in the images, and constrains the acquisition to a few meters from the seabed. The scattering phenomenon [56], due to suspended particles, is another phenomenon affecting underwater images, and is also affected by artificial lighting inasmuch as light rays collide with the suspended particles. As a result of these phenomena, underwater images suffer from poor and non-uniform illumination and frequently present bright spots due to backward scattering, and lack of sharpness due to forward scattering. The images affected by these problems make the detection of features and consequently the pair-wise registration difficult, giving rise at this point to the importance of the navigation data. The short distance between the camera and the seafloor favours the presence of parallax, which affects the 2D mosaicing approach due to the

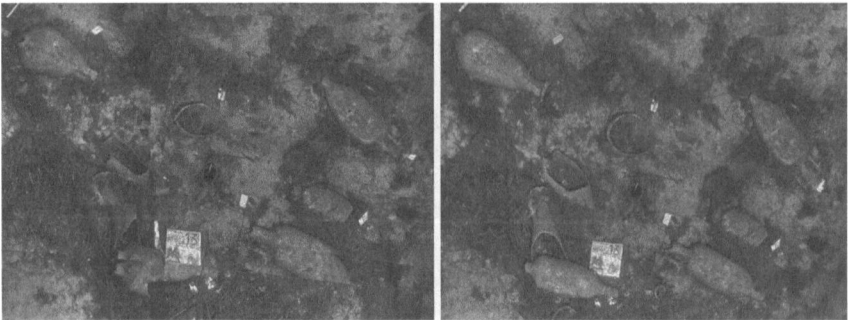

Fig. 2.6 Small area of a mosaic generated from an image set corresponding to a shipwreck in Pianosa (Italy). In the initial mosaic (*left*), before the application of a blending technique, the amphoras and white labels laying on the seafloor appear truncated. In the blended mosaic (*right*), the scene is easily understandable and the discontinuities have disappeared. Images courtesy of Pierre Drap (LSIS, CNRS)

violation of the planar assumption. The parallax effects, in addition to any moving elements in the scene, also impact image registration, and have consequences in the image rendering step. All these factors make the topology estimation and the global alignment [5–8], in conjunction with the use of the available navigation data, very relevant steps to achieve accurate photo-mosaics when dealing with thousands of images.

Given the heterogeneous appearance of the acquired images, and problems such as the planar assumption violation or the presence of moving objects, the use of image blending techniques is required. Apart from the visual appearance, blending techniques are also important for proper interpretation and scientific exploitation of seafloor imagery (e.g. [57, 58]). The structures, objects and areas of interest may cover a wide range of scales, from a few centimeters, i.e. microfauna or rocks, which would appear in individual images, to several hundreds of meters, i.e. topographic scarps or fractures, spanning several frames. The relevance of image blending arises at this point so that the photo-mosaics generated with these techniques present a consistent and uniform appearance (see Fig. 2.6). The blended photo-mosaic, where imaging artifacts have been minimized, allows us to analyze the features of interest, regardless of their size and imaging conditions.

Summarizing, the use of blending techniques in underwater 2D mosaicing is a crucial step when generating high-quality large-scale photomosaics. Preprocessing the images in order to correct non-uniform illumination and enhance their detail also becomes a key step in the mosaicing procedure. Enhanced images are best suited for the feature detection and correspondence finding steps. Providing the images with a good appearance is relevant not only from the aesthetical point of view but also from a functional one.

The problems of image blending and image quality enhancement are treated in the next chapters.

References

1. Szeliski, R., Shum, H.-Y.: Creating full view panoramic image mosaics and environment maps. In: Proceedings of the Annual Conference on Computer Graphics and Interactive Techniques (SIGGRAPH), SIGGRAPH'97, pp. 251–258. ACM Press/Addison-Wesley Publishing Co., New York, NY, USA (1997)
2. Sawhney, H., Hsu, S., Kumar, R.: Robust video mosaicing through topology inference and local to global alignment. In: Proceedings of the European Conference on Computer Vision, Freiburg, Germany, June 1998
3. Capel, D.: Image Mosaicing and Super-Resolution. Springer, Berlin (2004)
4. Gracias, N., Costeira, J.P., Santos-Victor, J.: Linear global mosaics for underwater surveying. In: Proceedings of the IFAC/EURON Symposium on Autonomous Vehicles (IAV), Lisbon, Portugal, July 2004
5. Ferrer, J., Elibol, A., Delaunoy, O., Gracias, N., Garcia, R.: Large-area photo-mosaics using global alignment and navigation data. In: Proceedings of the IEEE OCEANS Conference, pp. 1–9, Oct 2007
6. Elibol, A., Garcia, R., Delaunoy, O., Gracias, N.: A new global alignment method for feature based image mosaicing. In: Proceedings of the International Symposium on Advances in Visual Computing (ISVC), Part II, pp. 257–266. Springer, Berlin, Heidelberg (2008)
7. Elibol, A., Garcia, R., Gracias, N.: A new global alignment approach for underwater optical mapping. Ocean Eng. 38(10), 1207–1219 (2011)
8. Elibol, A., Gracias, N., Garcia, R.: Augmented state-extended kalman filter combined framework for topology estimation in large-area underwater mapping. J. Field Robot. 27(5), 656–674 (2010)
9. Elibol, A., Gracias, N., Garcia, R.: Fast topology estimation for image mosaicing using adaptive information thresholding. Robot. Auton. Syst. 61(2), 125–136 (2013)
10. Elibol, A., Gracias, N., Garcia, R., Gleason, A., Gintert, B., Lirman, D.: Efficient autonomous image mosaicing with applications to coral reef monitoring. In: Proceedings of the Workshop on Robotics for Environmental Monitoring held at IEEE/RSJ International Conference on Intelligent Robots and Systems (IROS), pp. 50–57, San Francisco, USA, Sept 2011
11. Brown, M., Hartley, R.I., Nister, D.: Minimal solutions for panoramic stitching. In: IEEE Conference on Computer Vision and Pattern Recognition (CVPR), pp. 1–8, June 2007
12. Szeliski, R.: Image mosaicing for tele-reality applications. In: Proceedings of the IEEE Workshop on Applications of Computer Vision, pp. 44–53, Dec 1994
13. Dani, P., Chaudhuri, S.: Automated assembling of images: image montage preparation. Pattern Recogn. 28(3), 431–445 (1995)
14. Horn, B., Shunck, B.: Determining optical flow. Artif. Intell. 17, 185–203 (1981)
15. Shum, H-Y., Szeliski, R.: Construction and refinement of panoramic mosaics with global and local alignment. In: Procedings of the International Conference on Computer Vision (ICCV), p. 953. IEEE Computer Society, Washington, DC, USA, 1998
16. Reddy, B., Chatterji, B.: An FFT-based technique for translation, rotation, and scale-invariant image registration. IEEE Trans. Image Process. 5(8), 1266–1271 (1996)
17. Wolberg, G., Zokai, S.: Robust image registration using log-polar transform. In: Proceedings of the International Conference on Image Processing (ICIP), vol. 1, pp. 493–496, 2000
18. Rzhanov, Y., Huff, L., Cutter, G.R.: Seafloor video mapping: modeling, algorithms, apparatus. In: Proceedings of the International Conference on Image Processing (ICIP), pp. 868–871, 2002
19. Rzhanov, Y., Mayer, L., Beaulieu, S., Shank, T., Soule, S.A., Fornari, D.J.: Deep-sea georeferenced video mosaics. In: Proceedings of the IEEE OCEANS Conference, pp. 1–6, Sept 2006
20. Lucas, B.D.: Generalized image matching by the method of differences. PhD thesis, Robotics Institute, Carnegie Mellon University, Pittsburgh, PA, USA, July 1985 (AAI8601180)

21. Lucas, B.D., Kanade, T.: An iterative image registration technique with an application to stereo vision. In: Proceedings of the International Joint Conference on Artificial Intelligence (IJCAI), pp. 674–679, 1981
22. Negahdaripour, S., Xu, X., Khamene, A., Awan, Z.: 3D motion and depth estimation from sea-floor images for mosaic-based positioning, station keeping and navigation of ROVs/AUVs and high resolution sea-floor mapping. In: Procedings of the IEEE/OES Workshop on AUV Navigation, Cambridge, MA, USA, Aug 1998
23. Negahdaripour, S.: Revised definition of optical flow: integration of radiometric and geometric cues for dynamic scene analysis. IEEE Trans. Pattern Anal Mach Intell. (PAMI) 20(9), 961–970 (1998)
24. Madjidi, H., Negahdaripour, S.: On robustness and localization accuracy of optical flow computation from color imagery. In: Proceedings of the 3D Data Processing, Visualization and Transmission (3DPVT), 2nd International Symposium, pp. 317–324, 2004
25. Negahdaripour, S., Madjidi, H.: Robust optical flow estimation using underwater color images. In: Proceedings of MTS/IEEE OCEANS Conference, vol. 4, pp. 2309–2316, Sept 2003
26. Negahdaripour, S., Xu, X., Jin, L.: Direct estimation of motion from sea floor images for automatic station-keeping of submersible platforms. IEEE J. Oceanic Eng. 24(3), 370–382 (1999)
27. Harris, C., Stephens, M.: A combined corner and edge detector. In: Proceedings of the Alvey Vision Conference, pp. 189–192, Manchester, UK, Aug 1988
28. Beaudet P. R.: Rotationally invariant image operators. In: Proceedings of the International Conference on Pattern Recognition (ICPR), pp. 579–583, Kyoto, Japan, Nov 1978
29. Lindeberg, T.: Feature detection with automatic scale selection. Int. J. Comput. Vision 30, 79–116 (1998)
30. Lowe, D.: Object recognition from local scale-invariant features. In: Proceedings of the International Conference on Computer Vision (ICCV), vol. 2, p. 1150. IEEE Computer Society, Washington, DC, USA, 1999
31. Bay, H., Tuytelaars, T., Van Gool, L.: SURF: speeded up robust features. In: European Conference on Computer Vision, pp. 404–417, (2006)
32. Haar, A.: Zur theorie der orthogonalen funktionensysteme. Math. Ann. 69, 331–371 (1910). doi:10.1007/BF01456326
33. Schmid, C., Mohr, R., Bauckhage, C.: Comparing and evaluating interest points. In: Proceedings of the International Conference on Computer Vision (ICCV), pp. 230–235, 1998
34. Hartley, R., Zisserman, A.: Multiple View Geometry in Computer Vision, 2nd edn. Cambridge University Press, Cambridge (2003)
35. Ma, Y., Soatto, S., Kosecka, J., Sastry, S.S.: An Invitation to 3-D Vision: From Images to Geometric Models. Springer, Berlin (2003)
36. Negahdaripour, S., Prados, R., Garcia, R.: Planar homography: accuracy analysis and applications. In: IEEE International Conference on Image Processing (ICIP), vol. 1, 1089–1092 (2005)
37. Huang, J-F., Lai, S-H., Cheng, C-M.: Robust fundamental matrix estimation with accurate outlier detection. J. Inf. Sci. Eng. 23(4), 1213–1225 (2007)
38. Fischler, M.A., Bolles, R.C.: Random sample consensus: a paradigm for model fitting with applications to image analysis and automated cartography. Commun. ACM 24, 381–395 (1981)
39. Rousseeuw, P.J.: Least median of squares regression. J. Am. Stat. Assoc. 79(388), 871–880 (1984)
40. Rousseeuw, P.J., Leroy, A.M.: Robust Regression and Outlier Detection. Wiley, New York (1987)
41. Li, X., Hu, Z.: Rejecting mismatches by correspondence function. Int. J. Comput. Vision 89, 1–17 (2010)
42. Szeliski, R.: Image alignment and stitching: a tutorial. Found. Trends Comput. Graph. Vision 2(1), 1–104 (2006)
43. Capel, D.P.: Image mosaicing and super-resolution. PhD thesis, University of Oxford, Oxford, UK, 2001

44. Marzotto, R., Fusiello, A., Murino, V.: High resolution video mosaicing with global alignment. In: Proceedings of the IEEE Computer Society Conference on Computer Vision and Pattern Recognition (CVPR), vol. 1, pp. 692–698, June–July 2004

45. Davis, J.: Mosaics of scenes with moving objects. In: Proceedings of the IEEE Conference on Computer Vision and Pattern Recognition (CVPR), Santa Barbara, CA, USA, June 1998

46. Kang, E., Cohen, I., Medioni, G.: A graph-based global registration for 2D mosaics. In: Proceedings of the International Conference on Pattern Recognition (ICPR), Barcelona, Spain, Sept 2000

47. Can, A., Stewart, C.V., Roysam, B., Tanenbaum, H.L.: A feature-based technique for joint, linear estimation of high-order image-to-mosaic transformations: mosaicing the curved human retina. IEEE Trans. Pattern Anal. Mach. Intell. (PAMI) **24**(3), 412–419 (2002)

48. Pizarro, O., Singh, H.: Toward large-area mosaicing for underwater scientific applications. IEEE J. Oceanic Eng. **28**(4), 651–672 (2003)

49. Shum, H.Y., Szeliski, R.: Construction of Panoramic Image Mosaics with Global and Local Alignment, pp. 227–268. Springer, New York (2001)

50. Morris, D.D.: Gauge freedoms and uncertainty modeling for 3D computer vision. PhD thesis, Robotics Institute, Carnegie Mellon University, Pittsburgh, PA, Mar 2001

51. Triggs, B., McLauchlan, P.F., Hartley, R.I., Fitzgibbon, A.W.: Bundle adjustment—a modern synthesis. In: Proceedings of the International Workshop on Vision Algorithms: Theory and Practice, ICCV'99, pp. 298–372. Springer, London, UK, 1999

52. Bouguet, J.Y.: Camera Calibration Toolbox. http://www.vision.caltech.edu/bouguetj/calib_doc. June 2008

53. McLauchlan, P.F., Jaenicke, A.: Image mosaicing using sequential bundle adjustment. Image Vision Comput. **20**, 751–759 (2002)

54. Gracias, N., Santos-Victor, J.: Underwater mosaicing and trajectory reconstruction using global alignment. In: Proceedings of the MTS/IEEE OCEANS Conference, pp. 2557–2563, Honolulu, Hawaii, U.S.A., Nov 2001

55. Elibol, A., Gracias, N., Garcia, R.: Efficient Topology Estimation for Large Scale Optical Mapping, Volume 82 of Springer Tracts in Advanced Robotics. Springer, Berlin (2012)

56. Shao, B., Jaffe, J.S., Chachisvilis, M., Esener, S.C.: Angular resolved light scattering for discriminating among marine picoplankton: modeling and experimental measurements. Opt. Expr. **14**(25), 12473–12484 (2006)

57. Barreyre, T., Escartin, J., Garcia, R., Cannat, M., Mittelstaedt, E., Prados, R.: Structure, temporal evolution, and heat flux estimates from a deep-sea hydrothermal field derived from seafloor image mosaics. Geochem. Geophys. Geosyst. **13**(4), 1–29 (2012)

58. Mittelstaedt, E., Escartín, J., Gracias, N., Olive, J.A., Barreyre, T., Davaille, A., Cannat, M., Garcia, R.: Quantifying diffuse and discrete venting at the tour eiffel vent site, lucky strike hydrothermal field. Geochem. Geophys. Geosyst. **13**, (2012)

Chapter 3
State of the Art in Image Blending Techniques

Abstract In this chapter the main state-of-the-art techniques are presented and described. There are three main groups of blending algorithms, each of them showing some benefits and drawbacks. On the one hand, transition smoothing methods minimize the visibility of the seams between two images fusing the image information of the common overlapping area. A drawback of this group of methods is that geometrical image misalignments and moving objects may cause the visualization of artifacts on the overlapping regions. On the other hand, optimal seam finding methods compute the optimal placement of the seam in order to minimize the photometric differences along the path. In the case of this group of methods, problems may appear when joining images acquired with changing illumination conditions or different time exposures. Finally, hybrid methods combine both strategies by fusing the image information around an optimally computed seam. This last group of methods allows avoiding the above mentioned problems. The chapter also proposes a classification of the methods of the literature based on their nature and capabilities. The aim of this classification is to discern the optimal strategy to blend large-scale high-resolution underwater photo-mosaics.

Keywords Image blending · Transition smoothing · Optimal seam finding

Stitching two or more images together to create a photo-mosaic that enables the interpretation of the benthos by a scientist (biologist, geologist, archeologist, etc.) requires the use of a blending technique to obtain a seamless mosaic (see Fig. 3.1).

Building a photomosaic requires performing a geometrical registration to align the images involved as well as a photometrical registration to equalize color and luminance appearances [1]. Both kinds of registrations may lead to image inconsistencies in the mosaic. The visibility of such inconsistencies should be minimized in order to provide the mosaic with a homogeneous appearance, which is important from not only the aesthetical but also the cognitive point of view. Geometrical misalignments result in distinguishable object discontinuities and incongruence, while photometrical misalignments make the visibility of seams more evident, reducing the consistency of the global appearance of the mosaic.

R. Prados et al., *Image Blending Techniques and their Application in Underwater Mosaicing*, SpringerBriefs in Computer Science, DOI: 10.1007/978-3-319-05558-9_3, © The Author(s) 2014

Fig. 3.1 Photo-mosaic built from six images of two megapixels. The mosaic shows noticeable seams in (*Left*), where the images have only been geometrically transformed and sequentially rendered on the final mosaic canvas, the *last image* on *top* of the *previous one*. After applying a blending algorithm, the artifacts (*image edges*) disappear from the resulting mosaic (*Right*). Images courtesy of Dan Fornari (Woods-Hole Oceanographic Institution)

Due to the above stated reasons, there are three main concepts guiding image blending algorithms. Firstly, the effects of different illumination or exposure times between images should be minimized. Secondly, an adequate seam should be found in order to reduce the visibility of micro-registration misalignments and moving objects. Lastly, a smooth transition along the selected seam must be applied to reduce the prominence of transitions between images.

The basic principles of image blending where established four decades ago [2] and include two main concepts which lead to two groups of algorithms [3]: *transition smoothing* and *optimal seam finding*. On the one hand, *transition smoothing* methods (also known as *feathering* [4] or *alpha blending* methods [5]) attempt to minimize the visibility of seams by smoothing the common overlapping regions of the combined images. On the other hand, *optimal seam finding* methods place the seam between images where photometric differences in their joining boundaries are minimal [6, 7]. Image blending methods often combine the benefits of both groups of algorithms (e.g. [2, 8]) in order to produce more plausible results and to reduce to an even higher degree the noticeability of the joining regions. A smooth transition between the fused images is applied, but along an optimally selected seam, a combination which helps to avoid double contours and blurring effects when image registration is not accurate enough. This group of methods will be called from now on *hybrid methods*.

This chapter provides a review of the most relevant blending techniques in the literature since 1975. The methods listed are divided into three different groups, corresponding to its main principle: *transition smoothing methods*, *optimal seam finding methods* and *hybrid methods*. A classification of the approaches according to several features and properties is also proposed in order to highlight their benefits and drawbacks in different scenarios.

3.1 Transition Smoothing Methods

The main concern of transition smoothing methods is to produce a non-perceptible transition between two images over a given overlapping region (see Fig. 3.2). The information of this common area is fused in such a way that the boundaries of the images involved become invisible. Even though a totally indistinguishable transition may be achieved, the content and coherency of the overlapping region is not guaranteed, as the information is fused without taking into account the content of the scene.

In the early 70s, D. Milgram [2] addressed the problem of the seamless combination of two satellite images. The approach was intended to deal with only one pair of images horizontally registered, which is a limiting factor for the application of the method to different and more complex scenarios. This constraint lead to a method which searches for the smoothest transition in a row-wise manner. An arbitrary surrounding range is defined at each row around a given selected seam pixel, allowing to smooth the transition in that direction using a weighted average of the luminance values. Consequently, the method achieves a smooth transition in the horizontal direction, but this smoothness cannot be guaranteed in the vertical direction. The weighted average of luminance values (of grayscale images) became the first approach to the transition smoothing problem and a basic principle used by several methods that arose in the following decades.

Still in the context of low-scale (order of mega-pixels) aerial photo-mosaicing, the limitation of using only two overlapping images was addressed in the first instance by Peleg [9], who introduced the concept of Seam-Eliminating Function (SEF). The SEF is based on a luminance smoothing function (i.e. a weighting map), obtained using a computationally expensive iterative relaxation algorithm, which is used to smooth the transition from an arbitrary number of overlapping images (although the overlapping information is not used and the seams used are not optimal), setting the intensity differences along the seams at zero. The main advantage of the method is that the gradual, smooth change does not affect the detail nor the picture near the seams. Nevertheless, in lack of an optimal seam finding strategy, images suffering from vignetting may lead to mosaics with noticeable illumination artifacts.

Fig. 3.2 Example of the
application of a transition
smoothing method on the
overlapping area of two
images. The images show
different exposures and significantly different sizes once
registered. As a result of the
blending algorithm, the transition between both images is
smooth though noticeable

In 1983, Burt and Adelson [10] introduced the concept of *image spline* to obtain a smooth transition among several images. The approach was multipurpose, extending its fields of application to any imaging scenario, as opposed to Milgram's [2] who focused on satellite imaging. It was also the first approach to image compositing, i.e., the first method able to seamlessly fuse several images from different and unrelated scenes. The images to be fused are decomposed into a set of band-pass component images, and a separate spline with an appropriate transition width is applied to each band. The goal is to fuse the features from the same scale at each band-pass level. Finally, the splined band-pass components are recombined into the desired mosaic image using a simple addition. The method suppresses the visibility of the seams and reduces the noticeability of the misalignments when registration is imperfect. However, it leads to double contouring and ghosting effects when the misalignment is significant (see Fig. 3.3). In 1996, Hsu and Wu [11] extended the idea of Burt and Adelson [10] by applying the method to wavelet subspaces with the aim of avoiding the undesired oversampling nature of the Laplacian pyramid. Although the improvement on the results obtained is negligible, similar results are obtained despite the higher computational cost.

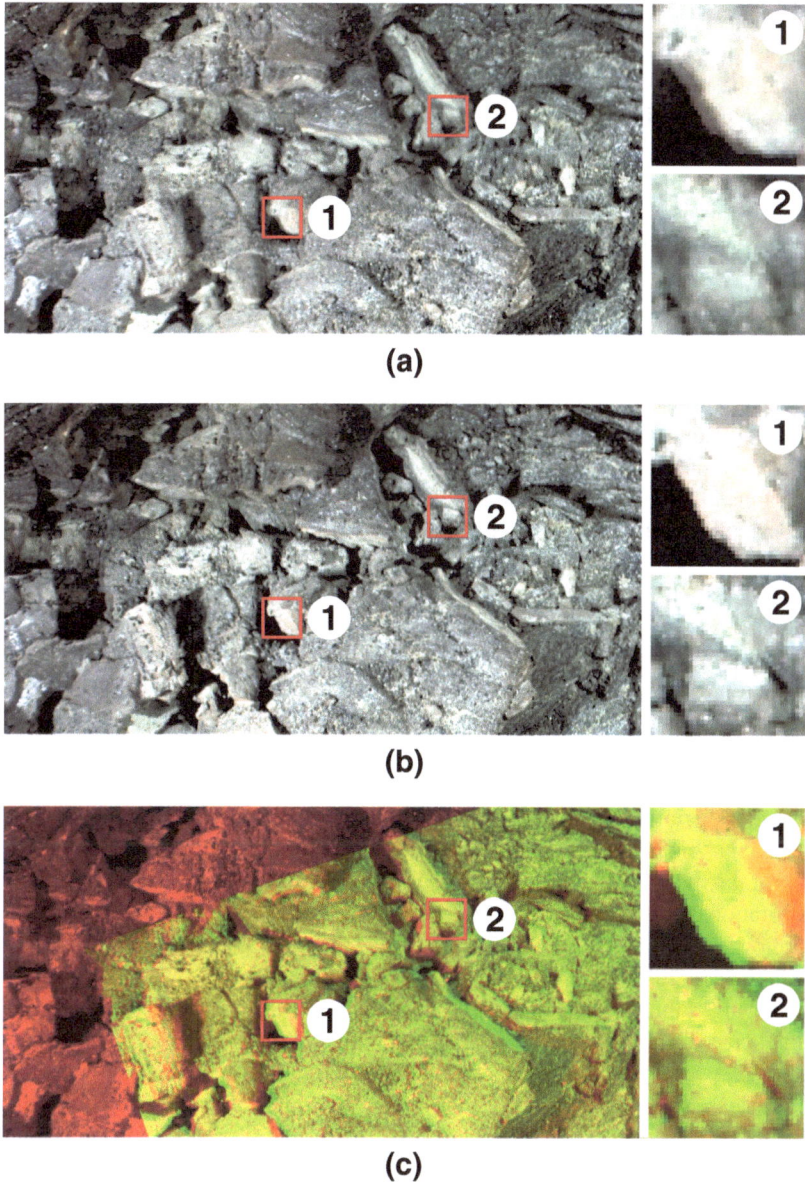

(a)

(b)

(c)

Fig. 3.3 Sample photo-mosaic region with (**a**) and without (**b**) ghosting and double contouring in the transition region due to registration inaccuracies. Seabed structures *1* and *2* are noticeably *blurry* in (**a**) while having a *sharp* appearance in (**b**). (**c**) shows *two overlapping* images of a given photo-mosaic (I_1 and I_2) represented in the *red* (I_1) and *green* (I_2) channels. Consequently, perfectly registered regions should appear in *yellow*, while the regions affected by misalignments present a *reddish* or *greenish* appearance. The image without ghosting and double contouring has been obtained using the blending approach proposed in this book. Images courtesy of Dan Fornari (Woods-Hole Oceanographic Institution)

In 2003, Pérez et al. [12] proposed a generic interpolation machinery based on solving Poisson equations for seamless editing and cloning of selection regions. Despite the main focus of that framework being image composition, it may also have applications in the underwater photo-mosaicing context when combined with an appropriate optimal seam finding strategy. The approach allows us to suppress the visibility of the seams along the joining regions. Beyond luminance and wavelet domains, this is the first important approach to image mosaicing in the gradient domain. The method is based on the idea that, through suitably mixing the gradient of a given image with that of another, it becomes possible to convincingly fuse image regions (namely objects) with a transparent appearance. The framework is based on the partial differential equation with Dirichlet boundary conditions which specifies the Laplacian of an unknown function over the domain of interest, along with the unknown function values over the boundary of the domain. As an extension of the technique presented by Bertalmio in [13], Pérez et al. proposed to modify the problem of image interpolation through Poisson equation by introducing further constraints in the form of a guidance field. In the same context, Levin et al. [3] proposed a method based in several cost functions for the evaluation of the quality of the stitching defined in the gradient domain. Levin et al. named GIST (Gradient-domain Image STitching) the framework developed based on this method. GIST provides two main approaches to image stitching. In the first one, images are combined in the gradient domain, reducing global inconsistences between the stitched parts due to illumination changes and variations in the camera photometric response. The stitched image is computed by minimizing a cost function evaluating the dissimilarity measure between the derivatives of the stitched image and the derivatives of the input images. In the second one, the mosaic image is inferred by optimization over image gradient, reducing seam artifacts and edge duplications. In this case, the stitching is performed using *feathering*, pyramid blending [14] or optimal seam [15]. The drawbacks of the methods working exclusively on the gradient domain are the important computational resources required to deal with large datasets.

Following the idea of gradient domain image blending, Agarwala et al. proposed a technique in 2004 that combined methods belonging to the two main classes of blending algorithms [8]. Firstly, *graph-cut optimization* [16, 17] was used to find the optimal place for the seam within the overlapping region. Secondly, *gradient-domain fusion* [12] was applied to reduce or remove any remaining visible artifacts along the image seams. The method has multiple applications in the image photomontage field and achieves convincingly seamless results. The framework developed was mainly intended to require user guidance to select the interest image regions, thus being unsuited for the automatic generation of photo-mosaics. In 2007, Agarwala [18] presented a hierarchical approach to improve the efficiency of gradient-domain compositing. The efficiency increase was achieved by observing that the difference between a simple color composite and its associated gradient-domain composite is largely smooth, and the pattern of this smoothness can be predicted *a priori*. This difference is solved by adaptively subdividing the domain using a *quadtree* hierarchical structure [19]. Unfortunately, the increases in efficiency with this method only occur if the problem can be transformed into a space where the solution is mostly smooth, and the pattern of this smoothness can be predicted *a priori*. Consequently, when the number of overlapping images increases and the overlapping regions become smaller, the performance of the methods also decreases. In 2011, Szeliski et al. [20] presented a technique for fast Poisson blending and gradient domain compositing which associates, to each input image, a separate low-resolution offset map, that can be represented using a low-dimensional spline. The resulting linear system is much smaller than either the original Poisson system or the quadtree spline approximation of a single offset map. Since each of the offset fields is represented using a low-dimensional spline, the resultant representation is called *multi-spline*.

Still in the context of gradient domain blending, Su et al. [21] proposed a method based on the minimization of a blending energy function, considering not only gradient values but also luminance. Within this blending energy function, indented to combine low-level image properties, two variation terms are measured and minimized: *image value variation* and *first derivative variation*. Image value variation measures the difference between corresponding pixel values of the images to be combined and the photo-mosaic itself. On the other hand, first derivative variations measure the difference between the blended values of each respective first derivative and the first derivative of the mosaic. The resultant image can be effectively obtained by minimizing the blending energy function. Unfortunately, the computational cost of the method (according to the authors, between six and eight times slower than [10]) makes it unsuitable for large image datasets.

The problem of stitching images in real time for online photo-mosaicing was addressed by Zhao [22] in 2006. The author proposed an efficient image blending method for creating good-quality and real-time dynamic image mosaics from an arbitrary number of input images. There are three main advantages with the flexible blending technique: (a) good results and possible implementation in embedded systems for real-time performance, (b) comprehensive treatment of geometry, time and user control and (c) capability of handling exposure imbalance among frames. Flexible blending has its basis in the sequential implementation of image blending features. Unfortunately, there are some drawbacks preventing its application in large scale underwater mosaicing. Firstly, the blending step is based on an improved multi-resolution weighted average [10] which prioritizes pixels close to the image centers, but does not offer good enough results when registration problems appear. Secondly, the exposure correction mechanism takes as a reference the exposure of the photo-mosaic built until a new image is added. This fact may lead to a global exposure degeneration when some of the implied images are over or underexposed. Lastly, the method is intended to deal with small input images, but its behavior when confronted with large input images sequences is unknown.

Few approaches in the literature have specifically dealt with the problem of underwater imagery mosaicing. Gu and Rzhanov [23], proposed as a blending step the application, around an optimally found boundary, of a pure gradient domain fusion of the boundary pixels only. The method claims to overcome the short comings of gradient domain fusion, which produce blurring in the case of misalignment inasmuch as is uses information from all the implied images to build the fused gradient field. The authors do not define a criteria for selecting the contributing image in the case where multiple images overlap the same region. Thus, [23] is limited to panoramic mosaics where only two images overlap over the same area. The color treatment is not performed, being assumed that the method is gray-scale intended.

3.2 Optimal Seam Finding Methods

The objective of optimal seam finding methods is to find an optimal placement for a seam line through a given overlapping region between two images (see Fig. 3.4). This seam should minimize the photometric differences on both sides of the line and determine the contribution of the involved images to the final mosaic. Unlike transition smoothing techniques, optimal seam finding approaches consider the content of the scene in the overlapping region, allowing us to deal with problems such as moving objects or parallax. In contrast, no information is fused, and the step between the images can be easily noticeable when illumination conditions or exposure times change from frame to frame.

Milgram [2] proposed a non-optimal seam definition strategy that searches the seam pixel offering the smoothest transition in a row-wise manner, inasmuch as it is intended to deal only with pairs of images horizontally registered. This random positioning of the edge was referred to as "feathering", and was claimed to help reduce visual cues, but with the disadvantage of introducing discontinuities in the vertical direction. In order to deal with this drawback, a restriction of the candidate seam points, depending on the magnitude of the minimum edge difference, was imposed. This restriction allows us to obtain a more continuous and consistent seam line. The same author later proposed an improved approach, adding a pixel selection criterion in the illumination compensation step in order to deal with shadows and moving objects and considering only the most informative gray level values [24]. Furthermore, a cost function was included in the seam definition strategy, permitting to control of the origin and the final pixel coordinates in the optimal seam path.

The problem of non-static objects in the overlapping regions was addressed by Davis [6] in 1998, who found an optimal seam using Dijkstra's algorithm [25] through the photometric differences computed between two registered images. The path obtained tends to cut around the moving object, leaving it either totally in or out of the final mosaic image. As a drawback, at least one image must contain a complete view of the moving object so as not to bisect it. Furthermore, some photometric issues that can disturb the seam localization, such as automatic exposure or vignetting, are not taken into account by the method.

Focusing mainly on the panoramic imaging context using a rotating camera, Uyttendaele et al. [4] proposed, in 2001, a method to suppress the ghosting effect in mosaic images due to moving objects, along with a procedure to adjust the exposure over multiple images to eliminate visible shifts in brightness and hue. The aim of the method is to deal with the complicated problem of multiple overlapping regions with moving objects. When confronted with ghosting artifacts, the authors proposed a search for Regions of Difference (RODs) in the overlapping areas in order to use

Fig. 3.4 Example of the
application of an optimal
seam finding method on the
overlapping region between
two images. The images
show different exposures and
significant different sizes
once registered. As a result
of the blending algorithm,
the transition between both
images is still noticeable due
to the different exposures and
different sizes, which leads to
a visible contrast concerning
detail richness

information from only one image per ROD. Hence RODs are defined in different images to be corresponding, i.e. to belong to the same scene object, if they have any overlap at all. Regions of Difference (RODs) are then used to build a graph in which the minimum weight vertex cover [26] must be computed. However, this method is not entirely robust and situations can appear where a wrong elimination of ROD causes holes in the mosaic image. Nevertheless, according to the authors, conflictive situations are rare in practice. Concerning the exposure artifacts, a block-based exposure adjustment technique was applied. The exposure compensation solution obtains smooth but still noticeable transitions between images in some cases.

In the context of image compositing, Agarwala et al. [8] proposed, in 2004, a technique which combined methods belonging to the two main classes of blending algorithms. Concerning the seam finding strategy allowing the selection of the image regions which will contribute to the composite, a *graph-cut optimization* [16] was used. This *graph-cut* was guided, depending on user preferences, by several features, such as color, luminance or likelihood, among others. The method has multiple applications in the image photomontage field and achieves convincingly seamless results. The framework developed was mainly intended to require user guidance to select the interest image regions, thus being unsuitable for the automatic generation of photo-mosaics.

Regarding the computational and memory cost reduction of Dijkstra's based optimal seam finding, Gracias et al. [27] proposed a method using watersheds and graph cuts intended to achieve execution speed when building large photo-mosaics. The use of watershed segmentation to find possible cuts over areas with low photometric differences allowed their algorithm to reduce the search to a smaller set of watershed segments, at the cost of sacrificing a certain degree of precision of the computed path, which is conditioned by the initial watershed segmentation. Furthermore, the use of graph cuts over image pairs guarantees a globally optimal solution for each intersection region. While the authors applied the algorithm developed to underwater images, the method can be extended to other contexts.

Eden et al. [28] presented, in 2006, a blending approach that included a two-step graph cut procedure to deal with both highly different exposures and misregistration problems, and work on a global radiance space for all the images involved. This is one of the first methods applied to the global radiance space domain. Firstly, the positions of the moving objects in the scene are defined (manually or automatically). Secondly, the entire available dynamic range is used to render the photo-mosaic. Therefore, a High Dynamic Range (HDR) image can be obtained from the photo-mosaicing process. Furthermore, two kinds of costs are introduced. Firstly, a data cost is computed to insure consistency and a high signal-to-noise ratio. Secondly, a seam cost is applied to favor smooth transitions. Nonetheless, such extreme exposure differences are not common in underwater photo-mosaicing. The gradient blending step is performed as in [8].

More recently, Mills and Dudek [29] presented a combination of techniques to create good quality image mosaics despite the presence of moving objects in the scene. The technique uses heuristic measures to determine the optimal seam, in both intensity and gradient domains, combined with a multiresolution splining [10] algorithm to refine the results around the selected seam. Concerning underwater imagery, the strong differences in appearance between images and the sequential nature of the approach may prevent its application. The exposure compensation of new added images is performed based on the already generated photo-mosaic, which may lead to mosaic degeneration as the amount of stitched images grows. Furthermore, the blending method used by the approach may lead to double contouring, specially in the presence of complex seabed structures.

In the underwater context, Gu and Rzhanov [23], similar to [3], proposed a graph-cut technique in order to select the optimal seam between two images, and the application of a pure gradient domain fusion around this boundary. The graph-cut is performed in the gradient domain with the aim of correctly dealing with images showing inhomogeneous illumination, but as opposed to [3], is performed on the overall image values, being more flexible in defining the cut area according to the authors.

Fig. 3.5 Example of the application of a hybrid method. A multiresolution spline [10] is applied around a seam determined by the distance from the pixels to the corresponding image centers in order to give more weight to the pixels close to the optical axis. The images show different exposures and significantly different sizes once registered. As a result of the blending algorithm, the transition between both images is smooth although not perfect, and the difference in detail richness between them is still noticeable

3.3 Hybrid Methods

The third group of methods, which we refer to as *hybrid methods*, is in fact not composed of any novel blending method, but of a set of appropriate *transition smoothing* and *optimal seam finding* techniques combinations. This group of approaches typically applies a transition smoothing method around an optimally calculated (or selected by some criterion) seam in order to improve the quality of the image regions joined reducing its noticeability to an even higher degree. As a result of the combination, problems such as blurring or double contouring presented by transition smoothing methods, and others such as different exposures presented by optimal seam finding methods, can be reduced or even totally avoided. One of the (evident) drawbacks of hybrid methods is their computational cost, inasmuch as at least two different strategies should be sequentially applied.

In fact, and as mentioned above, one of the pioneers in the image blending field, Milgram [2, 24], had already proposed, in 1975 and later updated in 1977, a hybrid approach based on the selection, in a row-wise manner, of an optimal seam (in terms of photometric differences) and the application around this seam of a weighted average, allowing a noticeable reduction of the image transition. Furthermore, a "zero-order" adjustment to compensate illumination differences between images was also used. This strategy was intended for satellite imaging and limited to grayscale images registered horizontally (regardless of rotation or scale changes). Nevertheless, it dealt with the most relevant concerns of image blending, i.e. the equalization of image appearance over a sequence (a pair of images in that case), the selection of a seam that minimizes photometric differences at the boundary and the application of a smoothing method around the seam to make the transition even less noticeable.

Agarwala et al. [8] proposed, as an optimal seam finding strategy, a graph-cut optimization [16] guided by several parameters, such as color, luminance or likelihood, among others. The transition smoothing in this case is performed in the gradient domain [12, 30]. Using the same labeling obtained after the graph-cut, the color gradients are used to form a composite vector field. The best-fit image in a least-squares sense is thereafter calculated by solving a discretization of the Poisson equations. Each color channel is processed independently, and in order to keep color channel coherency, the color of a given pixel is added to the Poisson equations to constrain the linear system. No overlap information around the boundaries is used, and according to the authors, in case of high-gradient edges, complications such as objectionably blurring artifacts may appear. In order to solve this problem, the linear constraints corresponding to these problematic pixels are removed. The gradient blending method acts in practice as an exposure compensation mechanism when all the images of the composite belong to the same scene. The approach of Agarwala is intended for image compositing, requiring human intervention when selecting the image regions to be fused, and consequently, is not suitable for automatic image mosaicing. Furthermore, performing the blending in the gradient domain regardless of any pixel overlap information, even if the equations corresponding to problematic pixels are dropped from the linear system, cannot guarantee a smooth transition in all scenarios.

Similar to Agarwala et al. [8], Eden et al. [28] combined the benefits of both an optimal seam finding strategy using a two-step graph-cut, and an optional transition smoothing method on the gradient domain. The main novelties of this approach are the use of a global radiance space for all the images involved, and the possibility of obtaining an HDR image as a result. In the first step of the graph-cut, the optimal boundaries are found in the same way as in Agarwala et al. [8] but in the radiance domain over a subset of geometrically and photometrically registered images covering the full field of view. After this step, the position of moving objects is defined, and can be manually changed or automatically selected. In the second step, an image selection strategy is applied, which determines the best radiance values in all the images of a given patch after the graph-cut in order to provide more detail, if possible, to the final composite. A secondary labeling is performed based on two cost functions; one determining the data cost of adding a given image pixel to the composite, and another determining the seam cost over each neighbor of this pixel. The goal of this second step of the image selection is to find the labeling of the final composite that minimizes both data and seam costs. Finally, the final composite can be obtained by either directly copying the corresponding radiance values into the final HDR mosaic after the graph-cut labeling, or applying a gradient blending of the original images using the Poisson equations [3, 8, 12]. Additionally, in order to visualize the final HDR image, a tone mapping algorithm is used [30–32].

Gu and Rzhanov [23] proposed, as an optimal approach for underwater image blending, a graph-cut strategy in the gradient domain in order to find the optimal seam placement, and a gradient domain blending as a transition smoothing method. The authors argued that performing a graph-cut on the gradient domain allows dealing with different exposures and inhomogeneous illumination more robustly than in the luminance domain, inasmuch as gradients are not affected by these factors. The gradient domain transition smoothing is performed in a similar way as [8, 12, 30], but applying a weight to a few pixels around the seam in order to reduce the artifacts caused by simple gradient blending, specially in presence of misalignments. In practice, the weighting leads to the usage of the average value of the gradients of pixels around the chosen seam. Nevertheless, this weighting is not able to get fully rid of ghosting artifacts around the image boundaries.

In 2009, Mills and Dudek [29] presented a full mosaicing approach to create pleasant and physically consistent image mosaics despite the presence of moving objects. The authors proposed performing a graph-cut along the differences between the luminance of two registered images in order to find an optimal seam. This graph-cut is computed, similarly to Davis [6], using Disjkstra's [25] algorithm. As a transition smoothing strategy, the multiresolutions splining of Burt and Adelson [10] is applied, which, in contrast to some gradient domain methods, uses the common overlapping pixels to smooth the transition. Inasmuch as the graph-cut is performed in the luminance differences domain, it cannot appropriately deal with different exposures or changes in the illumination conditions in the scene. On the other hand, the multiresolution splining strategy may lead to ghosting and double contouring in the case of misregistration, and cannot deal with different image exposures or illuminations.

3.4 Classification

The list of papers that form the state of the art in image blending is large, and the main requirements for conventional image panorama generation have been satisfyingly addressed by several of them. Unfortunately, blending in underwater photo-mosaicing is a specific application that has not been deeply treated in the literature. Consequently, not all the methods are appropriate for this context. In order to highlight the properties, benefits and drawbacks of the current methods, and to evaluate their suitability for underwater mosaicing, a classification is proposed.

There are several criteria that determine the behavior and performance of a given blending algorithm, including its capability of dealing with high resolution underwater photo-mosaics. Table 3.1 provides a comprehensive comparison of the most relevant blending techniques proposed in the literature. The specially important categories for underwater applications (mostly working with monochrome images) are

Table 3.1 Blending techniques comparison table

Method	Principle[a]	Domain[a]	Scalability	Color[a]	Dynamic range	Multi resolution	Real time	Sequential processing
Section	(3.4.1)	(3.4.2)	(3.4.3)	(3.4.4)	(3.4.4)	(3.4.5)	(3.4.6)	(3.4.6)
Milgram [2]	TS/OS	L	Low	GS	Low	No	No	Yes
Milgram [24]	TS/OS	L	Low	GS	Low	No	No	Yes
Peleg [9]	TS	L	Yes	GS	Low	No	No	No
Burt and Adelson [10]	TS	L	Low	CW	Low	Yes	No	Yes
Hsu and Wu [11]	TS	W	Low	CW	Low	Yes	No	Yes
Szeliski [33]	TS	L	Yes	CW	Low	No	No	Yes
Szeliski [34]	TS	L	Yes	CW	Low	No	No	Yes
Davis [6]	OS	L	Yes	CW	Low	No	No	No
Uyttendaele et al. [4]	OS	L	Yes	CW	Low	No	No	No
Hsu et al. [35]	TS	L	Low	CW	Low	Yes	No	Yes
Pizarro and Singh [36]	TS	L	Low	CW	Low	Yes	No	Yes
Pérez et al. [12]	TS	G	Low	CW	Low	No	No	No
Brown and Lowe [37]	TS/OS	L	Low	CW	Low	Yes	No	Yes
Jia and Tang [38]	TS	R	Yes	SC	Low	Yes	No	Yes
Levin et al. [3]	TS	G	Low	CW	Low	No	No	Yes
Agarwala et al. [8]	TS/OS	G	Yes	CW	Low	No	No	No
Su et al. [21]	TS	L	Low	CW	Low	Yes	No	Yes
Litvinov and Schechner [39]	RC	R	Yes	GS	No	No	No	Yes
Gracias et al. [40]	OS	L	Yes	CW	Low	No	No	Yes
Eden et al. [28]	TS/OS	R/G	Yes	CW	High	No	No	Yes
Zhao [22]	TS	L	Yes	CW	Low	No	Yes	Yes
Gu and Rzhanov [23]	TS/OS	G	Low	CW	Low	No	No	Yes

(continued)

Table 3.1 (continued)

Method / Section	Principle[a] (3.4.1)	Domain[a] (3.4.2)	Scalability (3.4.3)	Color[a] (3.4.4)	Dynamic range (3.4.4)	Multi resolution (3.4.5)	Real time (3.4.6)	Sequential processing (3.4.6)
Szeliski [41]	TS	G	Yes	CW	Low	Yes	No	No
Lempitsky and Ivanov [42]	TS	G	Yes	Yes	Low	No	No	No
Agarwala [18]	TS/OS	G	Yes	CW	Low	No	No	No
Nomura [43]	TS	L	Low	CW	Low	No	No	No
Cheng [44]	TS	L	Low	GS	Low	No	Yes	Yes
d'Angelo [45]	PC	R	Yes	SC	High	No	No	No
Rzhanov and Gu [46]	PC	L	Yes	Yes	Low	No	No	No
Suen et al. [47]	TS/OS	G	Low	Yes	Low	Yes	No	Yes
Kopf et al. [48]	TS/PC	L	Yes	Yes	Yes	Yes	No	No
Vineet and Narayanan [49]	OS	L	Yes	Yes	No	No	Yes	Yes
Wen and Zhou [50]	OS	HIS	Low	Yes	No	No	No	Yes
Szeliski [51]	TS/OS	G	Yes	CW	Low	No	No	No
Kim and Pollefeys [52]	RC	R	No	CW	Yes	No	No	No
Sadeghi et al. [53]	RC	L/G	Low	CW	Yes	No	No	Yes
Gracias et al. [27]	OS	L	Yes	CW	Low	No	No	Yes
Mills and Dudek [29]	TS/OS	G	Yes	CW	Low	No	No	Yes
Xiong and Pulli [54]	TS/OS	G	Yes	CW	Low	No	Yes	Yes
Xiong and Pulli [55]	TS/OS	L/G	Yes	CW	Low	No	No	Yes
Botterill et al. [56]	TS/OS	L	Yes	CW	Low	No	Yes	Yes
Johnson-Roberson et al. [57]	TS	L	Yes	CW	Low	Yes	No	Yes
Szeliski et al. [20]	TS	G	Yes	CW	High	Yes	No	Yes
Shao et al. [58]	TS	L	Yes	GS	Low	Yes	No	Yes
(2013) Proposed approach	TS/OS	L	Yes	CW	High	No	No	No

(continued)

Table 3.1 (continued)

Method / Section	Locality (3.4.6)	Ghosting removal (3.4.7)	Double contouring (3.4.7)	Exposure correction (3.4.7)	Moving objects (3.4.7)	Parallax robustness (3.4.7)	Application[a] context
Milgram [2]	Local	No	Yes	Yes	No	Yes	A
Milgram [24]	Local	No	Yes	Yes	No	Yes	A
Peleg [9]	Global	Yes	No	No	No	No	A
Burt and Adelson [10]	Local	No	Yes	No	No	No	A/IC
Hsu and Wu [11]	Local	No	Yes	No	No	No	IC
Szeliski [33]	Local	No	Yes	No	No	No	P
Szeliski [34]	Local	No	Yes	No	No	No	P
Davis [6]	Global	Yes	No	No	Yes	Yes	P
Uyttendaele et al. [4]	Global	Yes	Yes	Yes	Yes	Yes	P
Hsu et al. [35]	Local	No	Yes	No	No	No	IC
Pizarro and Singh [36]	Local	No	Yes	No	No	No	UW
Pérez et al. [12]	Local	No	Yes	No	No	No	IC
Brown and Lowe [37]	Local	No	Yes	No	No	No	P
Jia and Tang [38]	Local/Global	No	Yes	Yes	No	No	P
Levin et al. [3]	Local	No	Yes	No	No	No	P
Agarwala [18]	Global	Yes	No	No	Yes	Yes	P/IC
Su et al. [21]	Local	No	Yes	No	No	No	P/IC
Litvinov and Schechner [39]	Global	No	Yes	Yes	No	No	P/IC
Gracias et al. [40]	Local	Yes	No	No	Yes	Yes	UW/P
Eden et al. [28]	Global	Yes	No	No	Yes	Yes	P/IC
Zhao [22]	Local	No	Yes	Yes	No	No	A/P
Gu and Rzhanov [23]	Local	Yes	No	No	Yes	Yes	UW
Szeliski [41]	Global	Yes	Yes	No	Yes	No	P

(continued)

Table 3.1 (continued)

Method Section	Locality (3.4.6)	Ghosting removal (3.4.7)	Double contouring (3.4.7)	Exposure correction (3.4.7)	Moving objects (3.4.7)	Parallax robustness (3.4.7)	Application[a] context
Lempitsky and Ivanov [42]	Global	NA	NA	Yes	NA	NA	P
Agarwala [18]	Local	Yes	No	No	Yes	Yes	P
Nomura [43]	Local	Partial	Partial	Yes	Partial	Partial	P
Cheng [44]	Local	No	Yes	No	No	No	A
d'Angelo [45]	Global	No	Yes	Yes	No	No	P
Rzhanov and Gu [46]	Local	Partial	No	No	Yes	Partial	UW
Suen et al. [47]	Local	Yes	No	Yes	Partial	Yes	P
Kopf et al. [48]	Local/Global	NA	NA	Yes	NA	NA	P
Vineet and Narayanan [49]	Local	Yes	No	No	Yes	Yes	IC
Wen and Zhou [50]	Local	Yes	No	No	Yes	Yes	A
Szeliski [51]	Local	Yes	No	No	Yes	Yes	P
Kim and Pollefeys [52]	Local	No	No	Yes	No	No	P
Sadeghi et al. [53]	Local	Yes	No	No	No	Yes	P
Gracias et al. [27]	Local	Yes	No	No	Yes	Yes	UW/P
Mills and Dudek [29]	Local	Yes	No	Yes	Yes	Yes	P
Xiong and Pulli [54]	Local/Global	Yes	No	Yes	No	Yes	P
Xiong and Pulli [55]	Local	Yes	No	Yes	No	Yes	P
Botterill et al. [56]	Local	No	Yes	No	No	No	A
Johnson-Roberson et al. [57]	Local	No	Yes	Yes	No	No	UW
Szeliski et al. [20]	Local	No	Yes	Yes	No	No	P
Shao et al. [58]	Local	No	Yes	No	No	No	P
(2013) Proposed approach	Global	Yes	Yes	Yes	Yes	Yes	UW

[a]*TS* transition smoothing, *OS* optimal seam, *RC* radiometric correction, *PC* photometric correction, *LW* local warping, *L* luminance, *W* wavelet, *G* gradient, *R* radiance, *HIS* hue, intensity, saturation. *GS* gray scale, *CW* color wise, *SC* single channel, *A* aerial mapping, *P* terrestrial/landscape panoramas, *UW* underwater mapping, *IC* image compositing

exposure correction and elimination of *ghosting* and *double contouring*, concerning image quality, and *scalability*, concerning large scale photo-mosaicing.

3.4.1 Basic Principle

Two main groups of algorithms can be found in the literature in the context of image blending [3]: *transition smoothing* methods (also known as *feathering* [4] or *alpha blending* methods [5]) and *optimal seam finding* methods [6, 7]. The benefits of both groups of algorithms are combined into a third group, the *hybrid methods* [2, 8], in order to produce more plausible results and to reduce to an even higher degree the noticeability of the joining regions. Additionally, those methods avoid double contours and blurring effects when image registration is not accurate enough.

Each method uses a basic approach (*Principle*): *Transition Smoothing* (TS); *Optimal Seam Finding* (OS); or an appropriate *Hybrid* combination (OS/TS). The first set of methods (TS) often suffers from *Ghosting*, which concerns image blurriness of the finest details (i.e. low frequency image components), and *Double Contouring*, consisting in practice of a partial duplication of certain scene structures (i.e. high frequency image components), if registration is not accurate enough or the scenario considerably violates the planar scene assumption for 2D mosaicing. The second set (OS) is not able to deal with images with different *Exposures*, as is often the case in underwater imagery due to 3D relief, oblique terrain, variations in vehicle altitude, etc. Finally, *Hybrid* methods are able to compensate for these drawbacks to a certain degree.

Concerning the main *principle* of the techniques, the combination of a transition smoothing around an estimated boundary seems to be the most adequate approach and has been the most popular methodology in the literature since 2004, independent of the application context. The tolerance to *moving objects* is tied to this main principle. Optimal seam finding based methods naturally deal with this problem. In most cases, this tolerance is not actively treated, but is a result of the optimal seam search, which tends to make the cut in areas where photometric differences are small; overlapping areas with moving objects will thus be avoided.

3.4.2 Domain

The *Domain* in which the process is carried out (*Luminance/Radiance*, *Wavelet* or *Gradient*), has a double effect on the blending process. On the one hand, the image domain strongly influences the properties of the blending that will be performed. As an example, *Gradient* blending methods are able to unify different *Exposures* seamlessly and can lead implicitly to a high dynamic range from a set of low dynamic range images. However, *Gradient* methods require solving large sparse equation systems to recover the *Luminance* from the gradient vectors, and thereby their computational cost is significant. In contrast, *Luminance* based methods typically have lower computational requirements.

Luminance and gradient *domains* are widely used, and the second has become the preferred method in the latest publications [29, 51, 54]. This is due to the nature of the domain, which allows easy reduction of the exposure differences between neighboring images. Nevertheless, methods actively applying an *exposure correction* algorithm obtain more visually pleasant results. The ability to remove *ghosting effects* and the fact of presenting *double contouring* are complementary, and are avoided jointly.

3.4.3 Scalability

A particularly important property of blending methods is the *Scalability*, which we define as the ability to deal with more than two overlapping images. This property might be constrained by two main factors. The first one is the nature of the method itself, as in [2, 11, 24], which cannot work with more than two overlapping images. The second one is related to computational requirements: non-optimized *Gradient* algorithms suffer from poor computational scalability when the input dataset is extremely large, as in the case of Giga-Mosaics.

Leaving aside the first blending methods in the literature [2, 10, 11, 24], throughout the last decade most of the approaches have been scalable up to a certain point. Approaches such as [51] are intended to reduce computer requirements allowing the efficient processing of high resolution photo-mosaics. Unfortunately, these benefits only appear in the case of mosaics with images showing low overlap. In that case is possible to avoid storage and computations for image regions that remain unchanged after blending. This situation mainly happens in image panoramas, but not in underwater mosaics, where image registrations are unpredictable and geometrically non-uniform.

3.4.4 Color and Dynamic Range

Color is another critical factor when building visually plausible images. Colors change significantly as a function of the distance between the camera and the seafloor (known as robot altitude) due to the wavelength-dependent spectral absorption of the media. Mosaic blending techniques generally use a *Channel Wise* approach, where three color channels are processed independently and later reunified into a single color image. These methods have no control over perceptual color attributes. Several approaches in the literature address the color balancing problem in the image photo-mosaicing pipeline, based on exposure compensation in single [4, 37] or multiple channels [38, 59], and based on color transfer techniques [60, 61]. Unfortunately, dealing with extremely large datasets to generate photo-mosaics of large dimensions and keeping the consistency of the global image appearance is a difficult task when using methods available in the literature.

The treatment of *color* channels is common to all the methods in the literature, with the blending always being performed separately over each channel, independently of the number of channels of the source images. Consequently, a different smooth transition and location of the optimal seam are calculated for each channel. In this sense, Agarwala et al. [8] requires user intervention to specify some preferred color values, and [51] adds some constraints to the color variations in order to avoid significant color shifting. These corrections are performed channel-wise and do not treat the deep nature of the real colors. As a consequence, their performance when dealing with images evidencing different appearances due to light attenuation and illumination inhomogeneities is unpredictable.

The *Dynamic Range* of the image and the quantization of the data provided by the camera sensor strongly influence the accuracy of the final scene representation. Despite some of the methods reviewed being be able to work with high dynamic range images (with more than the common 8 bits per pixel and channel), they are not reported to do so. In fact, any *High Dynamic Range* blending method will require a *Tone Mapping* algorithm in order to display the *High Dynamic Range* mosaic image into a *Low Dynamic Range* device, such as conventional screens or printers [28].

Few blending methods claim to work with *high dynamic range* images. Nevertheless, gradient based blending methods are able to intrinsically deal with this kind of imagery, requiring the application of *tone mapping* algorithms to the mosaic image generated in order to visualize the results. A high dynamic range should be reduced so as to be displayed in low dynamic range devices.

3.4.5 Multiresolution

The use of a *Multiresolution* approach was first published in 1983 by Burt and Adelson [10]. Its main advantage is the significant reduction, but not suppression, of the noticeability of *Double Contours* due to registration inaccuracies. Under this approach, the images are decomposed into a set of band-pass components. For each different band, an appropriately selected width for the transition region T is applied, ensuring a smooth fusion at this spatial frequency band. An important shortcoming is that the method requires keeping several representations of the same image in memory, increasing memory requirements. The price of the seamless appearance is the loss of high frequency details. The *multiresolution* approach, based on the idea of Burt and Adelson [10], is applied by Su et al. [21] to the wavelet domain, but is the only variation of this idea in the literature.

3.4.6 Local/Global and Real-Time Operation

With respect to the *Locality* of the methods, *Global* methods require knowing all the final mosaic information *a priori* in order to perform the blending procedure, while *Local* methods can work on small parts of the final photo-mosaic, joining them together upon completion. Obviously, *Global* methods often require higher computational resources than *Local* ones, while *Local* methods may not be able to solve some problematic situations, such as loop closing, i.e. visiting twice or more a given scene region, or exposure compensation during a pair-wise sequential processing.

Methods that are able to deal with most of the mosaicing and blending issues in *Real Time* [22], though uncommon, are optimized towards high performance for large sequences. The results obtained are not as accurate as those from off-line approaches, but acceptable when on-line feedback is required. *Real-time* techniques are typically based on the *Sequential Processing* of the input data. Some methods, like Milgram [2] or Hsu and Wu [11], can process the images pair-wise and add the result to a final mosaic canvas. The pair-wise processing is a limiting factor for the scalability of these methods, which are not appropriate for sequences where a given place is visited more than once as the drift accumulated due to the sequential registration, without a global alignment correction, results in inconsistent overlapping regions. Methods that do not perform a *sequential processing* are better positioned to deal with problems like exposure compensation and ensure global appearance consistency.

3.4.7 Relevant Visual Performance Criteria

Different *exposures* between images are especially common in underwater imaging. Frequently, the AUV or ROV cannot keep a perfectly constant altitude (distance to the seafloor) during the survey, requiring the automatic adjustment of the *exposure time* between frames. The *exposure correction* might be performed *actively*, by pre-processing the image sequence to be blended, but may also be corrected by means of *gradient* domain techniques, inasmuch as this domain is not sensitive to time exposure.

As already pointed out above, *ghosting* and *double contouring* are mainly due to geometrical registration inaccuracies. When two overlapping images are not properly aligned, non-coincident features are smoothed, and thereby *ghosted*, when fused, while strong contours appear twice in the blended photo-mosaic. Underwater, the *forward scattering* phenomenon is responsible for loosing contrast [62] and, therefore, ghosting appears when merging images with significantly different depths (see Fig. 3.6). *Double contouring* underwater is sometimes unavoidable due to the limited camera distance to the seabed leading to *parallax*.

Moving objects often appear in underwater imaging, e.g. fish, algae, crustacea and other life forms or floating objects. Most of the *Optimal Seam Finding* algorithms

Fig. 3.6 Registration of two images acquired at significantly different altitudes. The image acquired at higher altitude shows strong light attenuation and scattering. These effects cause a noticeable different appearance between the two images

are able to deal with *moving objects*, actively or passively, and cut them out of the overlapping regions, keeping a single representation of each object in the final map.

Finally, the *parallax robustness* determines the ability of a given blending algorithm to deal with a sequence where the 2D assumptions were considerably violated. Underwater scenarios are characterized by frequent seabed depth-changes, as well as the direction of shadows produced by the artificial lighting systems of the AUV or ROV. *Optimal Seam Finding* techniques are typically the most indicated methods to deal with this problem.

The *parallax robustness* is strongly related to its tolerance toward moving objects, and methods able to deal with moving objects are often able to handle parallax. In fact, parallax robustness can be considered in practice as the ability of a method to avoid repeated objects or shapes.

3.5 Conclusions

The generation of terrestrial and aerial photo-mosaics from a set of images is a problem widely treated in the literature. The number of approaches confronting this problem is large and the main imaging issues, such as exposure variations, vignetting effects and the presence moving objects, have been mainly solved.

Nevertheless, the underwater medium presents additional problems which tend to make the common approaches fail when applied in this context. The problems of extreme non-uniform illumination, backward and forward scattering and parallax, in addition to significant exposure variations and frequent moving objects, are specific to the medium, and few approaches have been presented in that direction.

Consequently, a different processing pipeline is required to deal with all the problems affecting underwater imagery. This pipeline should also be computationally efficient to allow processing large data sets, whose images might be affected to various degrees by the underwater phenomena presented. Obtaining consistent high-resolution large-scale geo-referenced photomosaics is the goal of the developed pipeline, comparable in terms of visual agreeability to terrestrial and common aerial photo-mosaics.

References

1. Capel, D.: Image Mosaicing and Super-Resolution. Springer, Berlin (2004)
2. Milgram, D.L.: Computer methods for creating photomosaics. IEEE Trans. Comput. **24**(11), 1113–1119 (1975)
3. Levin, A., Zomet, A., Peleg, S., Weiss, Y.: Seamless image stitching in the gradient domain. In: Proceedings of the European Conference on Computer Vision (ECCV), Prague, Czech Republic, May 2004
4. Uyttendaele, M., Eden, A., Szeliski, R.: Eliminating ghosting and exposure artifacts in image mosaics. In: Proceedings of the International Conference on Computer Vision and Pattern Recognition (CVPR), pp. 509–516 (2001)
5. Porter, T., Duff, T.: Compositing digital images. In: Proceedings of the Anual Conference on Computer Graphics and Interactive Techniques (SIGGRAPH), pp. 253–259. ACM, New York, NY, USA (1984)
6. Davis, J.: Mosaics of scenes with moving objects. In: Proceedings of the IEEE Conference on Computer Vision and Pattern Recognition (CVPR), Santa Barbara, CA, USA, June 1998
7. Efros, A., Freeman, W.: Image quilting for texture synthesis and transfer. In: Proceedings of the Conference on Computer Graphics and Interactive, Techniques, pp. 341–346, August 2001
8. Agarwala, A., Dontcheva, M., Agrawala, M., Drucker, S., Colburn, A., Curless, B., Salesin, D., Cohen M.: Interactive digital photomontage. ACM Trans. Graphics (SIGGRAPH) (2004)
9. Peleg, S.: Elimination of seams from photomosaics. Int. J. Comput. Vis (IJCV) **16**, 90–94 (1981)
10. Burt, P.J., Adelson, E.H.: A multiresolution spline with application to image mosaics. ACM Trans. Graphics (TOG) **2**(4), 217–236 (October 1983)
11. Hsu, C.T., Wu, J.L.: Multiresolution mosaic. IEEE Trans. Consum. Electron. **42**(4), 981–990 (1996)
12. Pérez, P., Gangnet, M., Blake, A.: Poisson image editing. ACM Trans. Graphics (SIGGRAPH) **22**(3), 313–318 (2003)

13. Bertalmio, M., Sapiro, G., Caselles, V., Ballester C.: Image inpainting. In: Proceedings of the Annual Conference on Computer Vision and Interactive Techniques (SIGGRAPH), pp. 417–424, July 2000

14. Adelson, E.H., Anderson, C.H., Bergen, J.R., Burt, P.J., Ogden, J.M.: Pyramid methods in image processing. RCA Engineer **29**(6), 33–41 (1984)

15. Efros, A.A., Leung, T.K.: Texture synthesis by non-parametric sampling. In: IEEE International Conference on Computer Vision (ICCV), pp. 1033–1038, Corfu, Greece, September 1999

16. Boykov, Y., Jolly, M.P.: Interactive organ segmentation using graph cuts. In: Proceedings of the Medical Image Computing and Computer-Assisted Intervention, pp 276–286, 2000

17. Kwatra, V., Schodl, A., Essa, I., Turk, G., Bobick, A.: Graphcut textures: image and video synthesis using graph cuts. ACM Trans. Graphics (SIGGRAPH) **22**(3), 277–286 (2003)

18. Agarwala, A.: Efficient gradient-domain compositing using quadtrees. ACM Trans. Graphics (SIGGRAPH) **26**(3), 94 (2007)

19. Hanan, S.: Applications of Spatial Data Structures: Computer Graphics, Image Processing, and GIS. Addison-Wesley Longman Publishing Co., Inc, Boston (1990)

20. Szeliski, R., Uyttendaele, M., Steedly D.: Fast poisson blending using multi-splines. In: IEEE International Conference on Computational Photography (ICCP), pp. 1–8, April 2011

21. Su, M., Hwang, W., Cheng, K.: Analysis on multiresolution mosaic images. IEEE Trans. Image Process. **13**(7), 952–959 (2004)

22. Zhao, W.: Flexible image blending for image mosaicing with reduced artifacts. Int.l J. Pattern Recogn. Artif. Intell. **20**(4), 609–628 (2006)

23. Gu, F., Rzhanov Y.: Optimal image blending for underwater mosaics. In: Proceedings of the IEEE OCEANS Conference, pp. 1–5, Sept 2006

24. Milgram, D.L.: Adaptive techniques for photomosaicking. IEEE Trans. Comput. **C–26**(11), 1175–1180 (1977)

25. Dijkstra, E.W.: A note on two problems in connexion with graphs. Numer. Math. **1**, 269–271 (1959)

26. Chen, J., Kanj, I.A., Jia, W.: Vertex cover: further observations and further improvements. J. Algorithms **41**(2), 280–301 (2001)

27. Gracias, N., Mahoor, M., Negahdaripour, S., Gleason, A.: Fast image blending using watersheds and graph cuts. Image Vis. Comput. **27**, 597–607 (2009)

28. Eden, A., Uyttendaele, M., Szeliski, R.: Seamless image stitching of scenes with large motions and exposure differences. In: Proceedings of the IEEE Computer Vision and Pattern Recognition (CVPR), pp. 2498–2505. IEEE Computer Society, Washington, DC, USA, 2006

29. Mills, A., Dudek, G.: Image stitching with dynamic elements. Image Vis. Comput. **27**(10), 1593–1602 (2009)

30. Fattal, R., Lischinski, D., Werman, M.: Gradient domain high dynamic range compression. ACM Trans. Graphics (SIGGRAPH) **21**(3), 249–256 (2002)

31. Durand, F., Dorsey, J.: Fast bilateral filtering for the display of high-dynamic-range images. ACM Trans. Graphics (SIGGRAPH) **21**, 257–266 (2002)

32. Reinhard, E., Stark, M., Shirley, P., Ferwerda, J.: Photographic tone reproduction for digital images. ACM Trans. Graphics (SIGGRAPH) **21**, 267–276 (2002)

33. Szeliski, R.: Video mosaics for virtual environments. IEEE Comput. Graphics Appl. **16**(2), 22–30 (1996)

34. Szeliski, R., Shum, H.-Y.: Creating full view panoramic image mosaics and environment maps. In: Proceedings of the Annual Conference on Computer Graphics and Interactive Techniques (SIGGRAPH), SIGGRAPH '97, pp. 251–258. ACM Press/Addison-Wesley Publishing Co., New York, NY, USA, 1997

35. Hsu, S., Sawhney, H.S., Kumar, R.: Automated mosaics via topology inference. IEEE Comput. Graphics Appl. **22**(2), 44–54 (2002)

36. Pizarro, O., Singh, H.: Toward large-area mosaicing for underwater scientific applications. IEEE J. Oceanic Eng. **28**(4), 651–672 (2003)

37. Brown, M., Lowe, D.G.: Recognising panoramas. In: Proceedings of the IEEE International Conference on Computer Vision (ICCV), pp. 12–18. IEEE Computer Society, Washington, DC, USA, 2003

38. Jia, J., Tang, C.-K.: Image registration with global and local luminance alignment. In: Proceedings of the IEEE International Conference on Computer Vision (ICCV), vol. 1, pp. 156–163, Oct 2003

39. Litvinov, A., Schechner, Y.Y.: Radiometric framework for image mosaicking. J. Opt. Soc. Am. **22**(5), 839–848 (2005)

40. Gracias, N., Gleason, A., Negahdaripour, S., Mahoor, M.: Fast image blending using watersheds and graph cuts. In: Proceedings of the British Machine Vision Conference (BMVC06), Edinburgh, U.K., Sept 2006

41. Szeliski, R.: Image alignment and stitching: a tutorial. Found. Trends Comput. Graphics Vis. **2**(1), 1–104 (2006)

42. Lempitsky, V., Ivanov, D.: Seamless mosaicing of image-based texture maps. In: IEEE Conference on Computer Vision and Pattern Recognition (CVPR), pp. 1–6, June 2007

43. Nomura, Y., Zhang, L., Nayar, S.K.: Scene collages and flexible camera arrays. In: Proceedings of Eurographics Symposium on Rendering, June 2007

44. Cheng, Y., Xue, D., Li, Y.: A fast mosaic approach for remote sensing images. In: International Conference on Mechatronics and Automation (ICMA), pp. 2009–2013, Aug 2007

45. Pablo, A.: Radiometric alignment and vignetting calibration. In: Proceedings of the International Conference on Computer Vision Systems, 2007

46. Rzhanov, Y., Gu, F.: Enhancement of underwater videomosaics for post-processing. In: Proceedings of the MTS/IEEE OCEANS Conference, pp. 1–6, Oct 2007

47. Suen, S.T., Lam, E.Y., Wong, K.K.: Photographic stitching with optimized object and color matching based on image derivatives. Opt. Express **15**(12), 7689–7696 (2007)

48. Kopf, J., Cohen, M.F., Lischinski, D., Uyttendaele, M.: Joint bilateral upsampling. ACM Trans. Graphics (TOG), **26**(3) (2007)

49. Vineet, V., Narayanan, P.J.: Cuda cuts: fast graph cuts on the gpu. In: IEEE Computer Society Conference on Computer Vision and Pattern Recognition Workshops (CVPRW), pp. 1–8, June 2008

50. Wen, H., Zhou, J.: An improved algorithm for image mosaic. In: International Symposium on Information Science and Engineering (ISISE), vol. 1, pp. 497–500, Dec 2008

51. Szeliski, R., Uyttendaele, M., Steedly, D.: Fast poisson blending using multi-splines. Technical report, Interactive Visual, Media, April 2008

52. Kim, S.J., Pollefeys, M.: Robust radiometric calibration and vignetting correction. IEEE Trans. Pattern Anal. Mach. Intell. **30**(4), 562–576 (2008)

53. Sadeghi, M.A., Hejrati, S.M.M., Gheissari, N.: Poisson local color correction for image stitching. In: Proceedings of the International Conference on Computer Vision, Theory and Applications, pp. 275–282, 2008

54. Xiong, Y., Pulli, K.: Color correction based image blending for creating high resolution panoramic images on mobile devices. In: ACM SIGGRAPH Asia: Posters, SIGGRAPH Asia '09, pp. 47:1–47:1. NY, USA, New York, 2009

55. Xiong, Y., Pulli, K.: Fast and high-quality image blending on mobile phones. In: 2010 7th IEEE Consumer Communications and Networking Conference (CCNC), pp. 1–5, Jan 2010

56. Botterill, T., Mills, S., Green, R.: Real-time aerial image mosaicing. In: Proceedings of Image and Vision Computing New Zealand, pp. 1–6, Queenstown, NZ, Nov. 2010

57. Johnson-Roberson, M., Pizarro, O., Williams, S.B., Mahon, I.: Generation and visualization of large-scale three-dimensional reconstructions from underwater robotic surveys. J. Field Robot. **27**(1), 21–51 (2010)

58. Shao, H.-C., Hwang, W.-L.: Optimal multiresolution blending of confocal microscope images. IEEE Trans. Biomed. Eng. **59**(2), 531–541 (2012)

59. Tian, G.Y., Gledhill, D., Taylor, D., Clarke, D.: Colour correction for panoramic imaging. In: Proceedings of Sixth International Conference on Information Visualisation, pp. 483–488, 2002

60. Reinhard, E., Adhikhmin, M., Gooch, B., Shirley, P.: Color transfer between images. IEEE Comput. Graphics Appl. **21**(5), 34–41 (2001)

61. Xiang, Y., Zou, B., Li, H.: Selective color transfer with multi-source images. Pattern Recogn. Lett. **30**(7), 682–689 (2009)
62. Jaffe, J.S., Moore, K.D., McLean, J., Strand, M.P.: Underwater optical imaging: status and prospects. Oceanography **14**, 66–77 (2001)

Chapter 4
Proposed Framework

Abstract This chapter describes the full photo-mosaicing pipeline proposed in this monograph. This pipeline is intended to process datasets of thousands of images from large-scale underwater optical surveys. The first stages of the process involve the input sequence preprocessing, required to reduce artifacts such as the inhomogeneous lighting of the images, mainly due to the use of limited-power artificial light sources and the phenomenon of light attenuation and scattering. In this step, a context-dependent gradient based image enhancement is proposed, with allows equalizing the appearance of neighboring images when those have been acquired at different depths of with different exposure times. The pipeline follows with the selection of each image contribution to the final mosaic, based on different criteria, such as image quality and acquisition distance. Next, the optimal seam placement for all the images is found. A gradient blending, in a narrow region around the optimally found seam, is applied in order minimize the visibility of the joining regions, as well as to refine the appearance equalization along all the involved images. Finally, a novel strategy allowing to process giga-mosaics composed of tenths of thousands of images in conventional hardware is proposed. The technique divides the whole mosaic in tiles, processing them individually and seamlessly blending all of them again using a technique that requires low computational resources.

Keywords Image preprocessing · Inhomogeneous lighting compensation · Image enhancement · Gradient domain blending · Tone mapping · Giga-mosaicing

A full photo-mosaicing pipeline has been developed, conceived to address the most relevant specific problems of underwater imaging. Nevertheless, the application field of the proposed approach can be extended to the generation of conventional panoramas or maps from terrestrial or aerial images. Figure 4.1 shows the sequence of steps that are performed by our approach, which are intended to build high resolution blended photo-mosaics of the deep-seafloor.

R. Prados et al., *Image Blending Techniques and their Application in Underwater Mosaicing*, SpringerBriefs in Computer Science, DOI: 10.1007/978-3-319-05558-9_4, © The Author(s) 2014

Fig. 4.1 Full processing
pipeline of the proposed
underwater photo-mosaicing
approach. Some of the
processing steps can be
executed using parallel
computing techniques to
increase the performance of
the algorithm

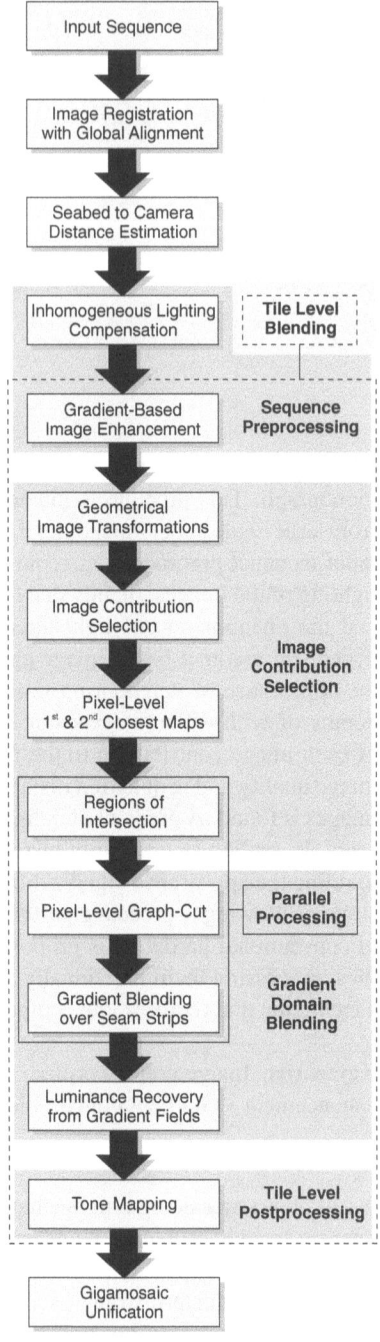

4.1 Input Sequence Preprocessing

Inherent underwater optical imaging problems have already been described in Sect. 1.2. Aside from *exposure variations*, which are a common issue in terrestrial images, other important problems are not directly addressed by conventional panorama generation software. To deal with these, image pre-processing is required, and is becoming a key step with a strong impact on the quality of the final photomosaic rendering.

4.1.1 Inhomogeneous Lighting Compensation

The *lighting inhomogeneity* problem in deep waters is mainly due to the lack of natural global lighting, and to the necessary use of artificial light sources with limited power. Illumination systems are often rigidly attached to the AUV or ROV and light sources typically concentrate the rays into a given area where the camera is focused. The acquired image borders suffer from darkening due to *light attenuation*, principally induced by the *light absorption* of the water. The effect is similar to *vignetting*, although the phenomenon is not produced by the camera lens but by the medium itself. All images from a given sequence are affected, to some degree, by this factor. The illumination distribution from artificial light sources changes with the distance from the camera to the seafloor. Colors are also affected due to *light absorption*, resulting in *depth-dependant* color profiles of the images acquired.

Imaging conditions hinder the application of a single compensation function on all the images acquired in absence of precise information about the placement and nature of the light sources, the distance from the camera to the seabed, and the 3D structure of the scene. This circumstance results in the loss of a global terrain perception, which is a cognitive sensation factor highly dependant on lighting coherency [1].

A feasible correction of *lighting inhomogeneity* and *vignetting-like* artifacts in a single step consists of the application of a 2D "inverse illumination distribution" to the original input images [2–5]. The main aim of this operation is to enhance the luminance of the darkened image borders in order to obtain uniform illumination throughout the image. If a high sensitivity camera with a high pixel depth (>8 bpp) is available, not only the luminance but also the richness of detail can be enhanced in the region affected by the *light absorption*.

The illumination pattern describing the "inverse illumination distribution" function can be estimated from a subset of images showing low texture and reduced 3D structure (i.e. flat, sedimented terrain). As this function changes with the distance from the light source to the seabed, a three-step approach is proposed (Fig. 4.2) to correct the lighting artifacts. It is based on two main ideas: (1) the application of a depth dependant inverse illumination distribution, and (2) the automatic selection of the images to compute this pattern in a given depth-range based on the Total Variation (*TV*) metrics [6], as described below.

Fig. 4.2 Lighting pattern compensation procedure. The images of a sequence are classified into depth subsets, and a different lighting pattern compensation function is computed for each one. The figure shows a set of *n* images from which the $n/2$ images having the lowest *TV* value have been selected. Next, the images are averaged and the result normalized and smoothed using a Gaussian filter with an adaptively selected σ

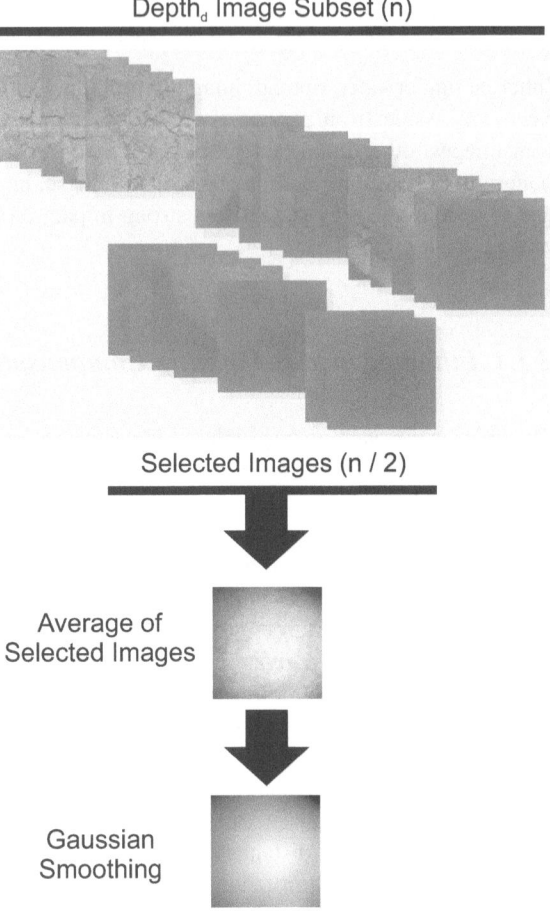

Quasi-Altitude Estimation

Underwater image acquisition platforms often record not only image sequences but also other synchronized data like heading, acoustic positioning, surface Global Positioning System (GPS) positioning and altitude, among others. Unfortunately, camera altitude is not always available for every data set. Consequently, as a first step, the images of a given sequence should be classified according to altitude in order to apply a different lighting correction function to each one, but assuming that precise information about distance from the camera to the seafloor may not be available. In order to solve that issue, a quasi-altitude estimation is now proposed to be used instead.

Given a sequence of images and its corresponding registration parameters onto the photo-mosaic frame, it is possible to determine which ones were acquired closer to the seabed and which ones further away by computing the size or scale of the image once registered to the 2D photo-mosaic coordinate system. Specifically, it is possible to consider only the diameter of the transformed pictures (i.e. the size of the longest diagonal) since this scale and the altitude are highly correlated when the focal length of the camera is assumed constant. Once an image list has been built and sorted according to their diagonal length, the images can be classified in subsets of similar altitudes.

Depth Sliding Window Strategy

The "inverse illumination distribution" changes with the distance from the camera to the seafloor, inasmuch as the light sources are rigidly attached to the UV. Consequently, this distribution should dynamically vary to compensate for depth fluctuations. In that sense, a depth sliding window strategy can be used. Given all the images of a given data set, the first step consists of sorting them by altitude, using sensor-acquired depth information or the quasi-depth estimation measure. The second step consists of opening a window centered on a given reference image in the sorted set with and arbitrary size depending on the frequency of the depth changes. The images in this window will be used to compute the "inverse illumination distribution" to be applied to the image on which the window is centered. With this strategy, a smooth variation of the function is ensured. Nevertheless, to avoid excessive computations, the step between reference images can be set to N instead of one image, and the function can be applied not only to the reference image but also to a small temporal neighbourhood determined by the value of N. In any case, this strategy will obtain an acceptably smooth variation of the function, in contrast with other strategies using a single function for all the images in the sequence, or those determining an arbitrary number of image depths.

Image Selection

For each image window, a distinct compensation function for the light distribution should be computed from images with a low texture content and homogeneous appearance. Low textured images are the best suited for this estimation due to their low average gradient length. An adequate ranking metric for the selection of these images is the TV.

$$TV = \frac{1}{W \cdot H} \sum_{x=1}^{W-1} \sum_{y=1}^{H-1} \|g(x, y)\| \tag{4.1}$$

Equation 4.1 shows the computation of the normalized TV for a given image, where W and H are the width and height sizes and $\|g\|$ notates the L_1 or L_2 norm of the g gradient vector. The TV values for the last row and column of a given image are set to 0.

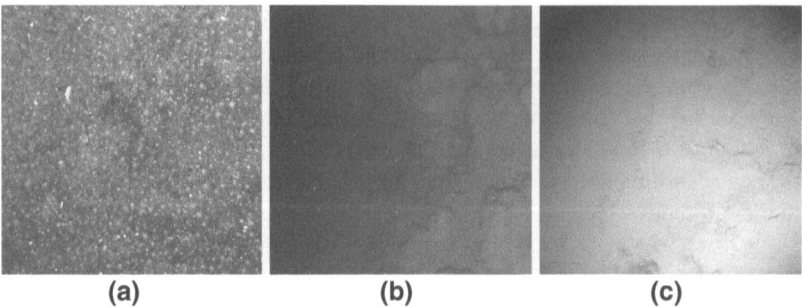

Fig. 4.3   a Example of *back-scattering* due to the reflection of rays from the light source on particles in suspension, hindering the identification of the seafloor texture. **b** Example of *forward scattering* caused by the local inter-reflection of the light suspended particles, hiding the terrain behind them. **c** Effects produced by *light absorption* of the water resulting in an evident loss of luminance in the regions farther from the focus of the artificial lighting

Equation 4.1 can be used with both L_1 or L_2 norms. In our experiments, we have selected the L_2 norm, i.e. Euclidean metrics, to evaluate the homogeneity of the images, because it allows characterizing the magnitude of the neighboring pixel variations (i.e. gradient vectors). Once the *TV* measure has been computed for all the images of a given altitude subset, an image subset of low *TV* is used to estimate the light distribution. The aim of the measure is to identify images containing structures rich in details. The presence of high frequency noise, mainly due to scattering on macroscopical particles in suspension of scattering (see Fig. 4.3), may skew the image quality evaluation. The *TV* magnitude of the image may inappropriately increase leading to scenarios where the dominant part of the metrics comes from high frequency noise. Nevertheless, the unwanted effects of the high frequency components can be avoided by building lower resolution images from the originals with $N \times N$ super-pixels. This simple approach significantly reduces the effects of the high frequency components in both the image and the *TV* measure. In practice, 8×8 linearly averaged super-pixels may produce good results for images of $1{,}024 \times 1{,}024$ pixels, which are reduced to 128×128 pixels. The images obtained save every important seabed feature but cancel the effects of the scattering phenomena, allowing the use of the *TV* as an image quality evaluation metrics. For each depth-range, the images with a *TV* value below the median can be used to compute the illumination correction function. To obtain this function, the selected images are averaged and the result is smoothed by a low-pass filter to reduce the remaining high frequency components, as explained below.

Compensation of Lighting Inhomogeneities

In order to compensate the light attenuation problems and obtain an image with a homogeneous illumination l_H, the acquired luminance values are divided by a given compensation mask as shown in Eq. 4.2

$$l_H(x, y) = \frac{l(x, y)}{l_G(x, y)} \tag{4.2}$$

where l is the image luminance values, l_G corresponds to the illumination pattern and l_C is the lighting compensation pattern before the Gaussian smoothing.

$$l_C(x, y) = \frac{1}{N} \sum_{k=1}^{N} l_k(x, y) \tag{4.3}$$

Equation 4.3 computes the average value for every pixel position given a stack of N images. Finally, the compensation mask l_C obtained is smoothed with a low-pass Gaussian filter to obtain the illumination distribution l_G function. This distribution is then used for the *lighting inhomogeneity* compensation, as per Eq. 4.4, where $\langle \rangle$ denotes Gaussian smoothing.

$$l_G(x, y) = \langle l_C \rangle \tag{4.4}$$

The value for σ used in the Gaussian convolution is selected adaptively for each altitude subset. Starting from the average image l_C in Eq. 4.3, a set of increasing values $\sigma_1, \sigma_2, \ldots, \sigma_k$ will be sequentially applied to it until the smoothed TV value is under a threshold $TV(l_{G(\sigma)}) < \varepsilon$. Values in the range of $\frac{d}{256}, \frac{d}{128}, \ldots, \frac{d}{32}$, where d is the shortest dimension of a given image, offer good results in practice. With this threshold condition the appropriate smoothness and uniformity of the blurred image are ensured.

4.1.2 Gradient-Based Image Enhancement

As the altitude of the robot increases, the effects of the previously mentioned *back-scattering*, *forward scattering* and *light absorption* phenomena become more evident. The strategy proposed to enhance the high frequency details affected by these phenomena is a simple and global approach, selecting the highest quality image in a given surrounding region from the whole set, and using it as a contrast or gradient reference. To avoid unpredictable visual effects, the non-global approaches of homomorphic filtering [7, 8], Contrast Limited Adaptive Histogram Equalization (CLAHE) [9] (Fig. 4.4) and histogram specification [10] are not used, due to the following reasons. On the one hand, homomorphic filtering may lead to an excessively homogeneous appearance of the filtered image and to a loss of global consistency in the appearance of the photo-mosaic. The suppression of low frequencies performed by this kind of filter may provide some advantages in the visibility of local details, but in giga-mosaicing, depending on the zoom factor, every spatial frequency can be important to recognize and understand the nature and morphological attributes

Fig. 4.4 (*Top-left*) Image lacking contrast on its *left side*. (*Top-right*) Image processed with a CLAHE algorithm, showing enhanced details in the originally lower-contrast regions. sssThe appearance of the processed image is less realistic than the original due to an aggressive level of local filtering. (*Bottom-left*) Image processed with a Butterworth homomorphic filter. The image evidences a generalized lack of contrast. (*Bottom-right*) Image resulting from the histogram specification of an apparently uniformly illuminated image into the test image. The image obtained has better contrast than the original, but still evidences problems in the *darkest* areas

of the seabed structures. On the other hand, histogram specification is highly dependent on the reference image, and therefore the modified image may often loose its realistic appearance. Therefore a simple but robust local contrast stretching can be applied to equalize a given sequence of images.

Image Quality Estimation

There is not a single and objective criterion to identify the image with the highest visual quality from a given set because the concept of "quality" involves different cognitive aspects. However, phenomena affecting image detail richness and sharpness, such as *scattering* and *light absorbtion*, are known to grow with the distance from the camera to the seabed.

This simple and fast approach may lead to poor results when the selected image presents an over-exposed region, for example, due to being acquired too close to the seabed under strong illumination. A more robust selection of the reference image is to use *TV* to rank image quality also. Thus, the image with the highest *TV* may be selected as the reference image while ensuring that over-exposed regions do not affect this selection. According to our experimental validation, the image with the highest *TV* coincides in most cases with the closest one to the seabed on a given survey, and with the second or the third closest images in the few remaining cases.

Global Contrast Stretching

The *TV* value of the reference image selected is used to compute the stretching factors that will be applied for a global contrast (or gamma amplification) on all the other images. This stretching factor should be selected below a given threshold T_s to avoid overamplification of areas of poor contrast, e.g. textureless sediment-covered regions. T_s depends on the Signal-to-Noise Ratio (SNR) of the image, which can vary highly according to water quality, lighting intensity, and/or the camera sensor. Despite the application of these gradient corrections, the merging of images from highly different depth categories will unavoidably produce noticeable seams due to their distinct blurring levels. The stretching factor $\frac{TV_{reference}}{TV(k)}$ is applied to enhance the x and y gradient components of the k-th image.

4.2 Image Registration with Global Alignment

While image registration is not directly related to the blending procedure and, therefore, is not at the core of the work presented here, the accuracy of image registration will significantly affect the final quality of the photo-mosaic rendered.

Even when navigation data (such as USBL positioning, heading, depth, etc.) are available, pair-wise image registration is still required to ensure a precise camera motion estimation. Pair-wise registration can be performed using a feature-based approach, involving the well known image feature detectors and descriptors of Harris [11], SIFT [12] and SURF [13], among others. When building a 2D photo-mosaic from a set of images acquired by a camera close to the seabed, the *planar assumption* of the scene can be violated due to the microbathymetry of the seafloor.

As already stated in Sect. 2.3.2. The 3D geometry of the scene, in addition to the short camera distance, results in *parallax*. This problem increases the difficulty of estimating the 2D planar transformation between consecutive images, often leading to *misregistrations*, resulting in double contour effects during blending.

A global alignment strategy [14, 15] is required to reduce the inaccuracies of a simple sequential pair-wise registration, as explained in Sect. 2.4. The strength of the global alignment arises from closing-loops because they allow a significant improvement of the camera trajectory estimate when re-visiting an already mapped area. In absence of loop-closings, and considering input sequences of thousands of images, the drift accumulated by the pair-wise transformations leads to significantly inconsistent (missaligned) photo-mosaics.

4.3 Image Contribution Selection

The *parallax* effect will influence both image registration and image blending procedures. On the one hand, image panorama software often fails to register sequences with strong *parallax* since they assume camera rotation only. On the other hand, and even using the best possible registration, the double contouring problem will appear when merging two or more images if the vehicle (and the camera) translates and the scene is not perfectly planar.

The solution to avoid ghosting artifacts is the use of information from a single image for each pixel of the final photo-mosaic whenever possible. Blending is performed in a narrow region around the optimally computed seams, and consequently information from more than one image is fused only in a small fraction of the final photo-mosaic. Ghosting may occur in those regions, but its noticeability is significantly localized and dependent on the width of the transition region.

4.3.1 Image Discarding

Each pixel of the photo-mosaic is obtained from a single image pixel whenever possible. To maximize the quality of the final photo-mosaic, the contribution from sharper and informative images should be prioritized. Image blending algorithms take into account the information of all the available images. Unfortunately, this may lead to unnecessary contributions of low quality images even when higher quality information is available in a given area. Therefore, discarding low quality images will ensure that their information is not taken into account in any sense. Furthermore, ignoring these images will also impact the optimal seam finding step, reducing the number of paths to be computed, and consequently speeding up the process. The developed discarding procedure is described below.

First, the frames of the original images are mapped into the global photo-mosaic frame using the image registration parameters in order to know their shape and area coverage in the final photo-mosaic coordinate system. The depth estimation is computed, assuming that depth information is not available in the navigation data. It is possible to discard low quality images covering a region of the scene if higher quality ones are available for that area. The discarding procedure is performed using logical operations on the polygons describing the images, which is an efficient approach requiring few resources.

Each image is defined as a trapezoid described by four vertices corresponding to the four image corners once registered to the photo-mosaic frame. Additionally, the polygons are sorted decreasingly according to their corresponding image TV value. At each step of the iterative process, a new image trapezoid of the sorted list is added to the final photo-mosaic polygon using simple binary operators. If the area covered by the new trapezoid has already been fully covered by the photo-mosaic polygon (i.e. the trapezoid does not intersect the photo-mosaic polygon and lies inside this one), the image is discarded because this same region is supposed to have already been covered by higher quality images. Otherwise, if the image to be added contains information from a non-covered area, the photo-mosaic polygon is updated and the image is accepted.

4.3.2 Pixel-Level First-Closest and Second-Closest Maps

The proposed blending methodology determines the first and second closest maps at pixel level. The *first closest map* contains, for each pixel coordinate of the photo-mosaic, the index of the image whose center is closest (see Fig. 4.5). The *second closest map* does the same, but with the second closest image indices. Similar to [16], the overlap of these two maps will use a graph-cut algorithm to compute the seam-strips for blending. For every *seam pixel* two image indices are selected. Therefore, every pixel outside the seams (most of the photo-mosaic) is associated to a single image.

The Euclidean distance between a pixel $I^M(x, y)$ in the photo-mosaic frame and the center of a given n-th image $I^n(x, y)$ is weighted by a factor $w_n(s)$, as shown in Eq. 4.5:

$$d_M^n(x, y) = w_n(s) \cdot \sqrt{(x_M - x_n)^2 + (y_M - y_n)^2} \qquad (4.5)$$

where the scalar factor $w_n(s)$ is a size-ratio between the n-th image and the image having the smallest area once registered. For time efficiency reasons, the ratio is not computed based on the area of the warped images, but on the length of their diameters, as explained in Sect. 4.1.1, to obtain a rough but fast approximation, as shown in Eq. 4.6:

$$w_n(s) = s_{\min}/s_n \qquad (4.6)$$

where $s_{\min}$ is the diameter of the smallest image for a given set and s_n is the diameter of a given n-th image.

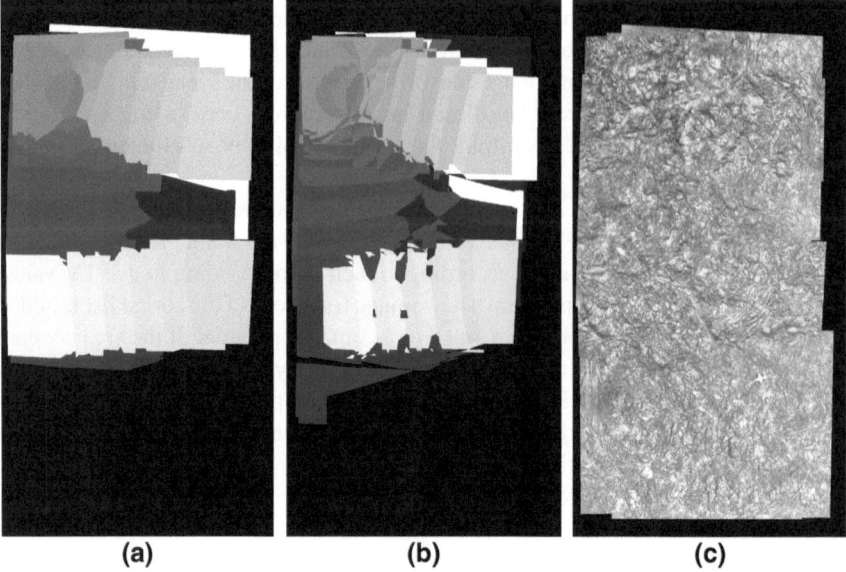

(a)   **(b)**   **(c)**

Fig. 4.5 a First closest map and **b** second closest map corresponding to the registered images
finally blended into the **c** photo-mosaic. The *blue* level of every pixel in the closest maps represents
the index of the image having the closest and second closest image centers. The distance measure
gives more priority to pixels belonging to images which have been acquired at a lower altitude,
consequently showing a higher level of detail

This weighting prioritizes pixels from images acquired at low altitudes, close to
the seabed, and consequently less affected by underwater imagery artifacts. This
weighting also maximizes the contribution of "higher-quality" images to the final
photo-mosaic image. Therefore, in cases like the one shown in Fig. 4.6, only a small
percentage of the pixels from the smaller overlapping image are lost while computing
the smooth transition, while the most significant percentage of the original image is
preserved.

4.3.3 Regions of Intersection

The overlap between the first and second closest maps determines the regions where
the pixel level graph cut should be performed. Therefore, for each overlapping patch,
the texture from the two best-quality images is available, and the graph cut is used
to find the optimal boundary seam, determining the contribution of each one in the
final photo-mosaic. Each region of intersection $ROI_{i,j}$ between the two images i and
j, where i is the closest image, j is the second closest image, and $R_{i,j}$ denotes the
photo-mosaic region where i and j coincide, is defined as $ROI_{i,j} = R_{i,j} \cup R_{j,i}$.

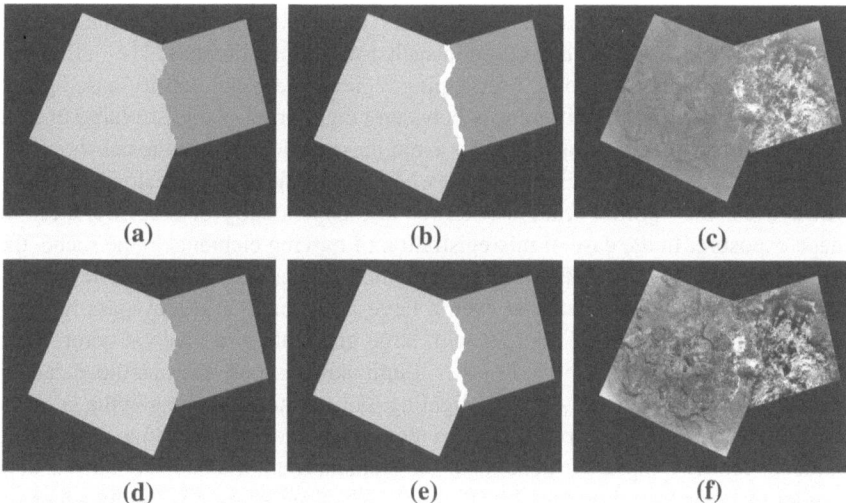

Fig. 4.6 Example of a pixel level graph-cut performed between two overlapping images acquired at different altitudes, and consequently evidencing differences in appearance. **a** Result of the graph cut performed on the images without enhancement, **b** depicts, in *white*, the narrow strip (20 pixels on each side of the cut) where the gradient domain blending is performed and **c** shows the blended image pair. **d** is the result of the graph cut performed on the images after being enhanced according to the proposed neighboring based enhancement approach, **e** depicts, in *white*, the narrow strip where the gradient domain is performed and **f** shows the blended image pair. Notice that the results of the pixel-level graph-cuts are different before and after the application of the image enhancements

4.4 Gradient Domain Blending

4.4.1 Pixel-Level Graph-Cut

The proposed blending strategy uses an optimal seam finding algorithm to compute the best boundaries in the overlapping image areas. A pixel level graph cut is performed on the regions of intersection determined by the first and second closest maps. In contrast to [16], the graph-cut is performed at the pixel level in order to guarantee maximum accuracy of the cut, given that the main aim of the algorithm is to achieve a high image quality. The algorithm searches for the boundary that minimizes the cost of the transition from one side to the other of the border line for every pair of pixels. The function has three weighted terms controlling the behavior of the cut:

$$C = \mu_1 \cdot f(I_1, I_2) + \mu_2 \cdot s(g_1, g_2) + \mu_3 \cdot L \qquad (4.7)$$

The first term $\mu_1 \cdot f(I_1, I_2)$ measures the intensity differences between overlapping pixels. The second term $\mu_2 \cdot s(g_1, g_2)$ measures the gradient vector differences along the boundary B seam. Finally, the third term $\mu_3 \cdot L$ measures the length L of the seam. The three weighting factors μ_1, μ_2 and μ_3 control the behavior of the cut. The gradient term, which is not been used in such a way in the literature [16], allows us to deal with differently exposed overlapping regions. Here an intensity-based graph cut will consider that the differences between neighboring pixels are large even if the registration is accurate, and thereby avoid those regions where the cut should be performed. Instead, if the difference between the gradient vectors along the seam path is used, the optimal seam will be found independently of the differences of image exposure. In the case of misregistration of moving elements in the scene, the term $\mu_2 \cdot s(g_1, g_2)$ avoids bisecting those elements by having the seam line by-pass them. This is due to the fact that even a large value of L in the by-pass has less cost than crossing a double contour with large gradients of a given structure. The gradients are also less sensitive to other illumination issues, such as those caused by artificial lighting and non-uniform lighting. Furthermore, working in the gradient domain compensates the exposures when recovering the luminance images from the gradient vectors. Despite the benefits of the gradient term, the intensity term is kept in order to favor low photometric differences when registration is highly accurate. Therefore, a weighted addition between both intensity and gradient domain terms is proposed.

The effects of *parallax* and registration inaccuracies are minimized since the graph cut tends to place the seam in textureless regions where morphological differences are low. For the same reason, cuts over moving objects tend to be avoided, thus benefiting the visual consistency of the blended results.

Performing a graph cut, especially at pixel level, is usually a computationally expensive operation when the size of the region to process is significantly large. Nevertheless, the regions on which the graph cut is working, determined by the intersection between the first and second closest maps, are rarely large. Furthermore, this process can be parallelized, taking advantage of recent multi-core processors, to speed up the execution in one of the main bottlenecks of the processing pipeline.

4.4.2 Gradient Blending Over Seam Strips

Once an optimal seam has been estimated, a smooth transition between neighboring regions needs to be performed. Even for sequences where the images have been preprocessed to solve non-uniform illumination problems such exposure artifacts and contrast level equalization, the graph cut result may lead to an image with noticeable seams. Therefore, smoothing the transition between the image patches is required. The image fusion around the computed seams should be performed in a limited region, being both wide enough to ensure a smooth transition and narrow enough to reduce the noticeability of ghosting and double contouring. According to our experience, a transition strip of 10 pixels at each side of the seam (i.e. a 20 pixels transition region) has been demonstrated to be appropriate for sequences of 1-Mpixel images.

A new transition smoothing approach is proposed in this book. The applied method is a weighted average around the seams in the gradient domain, as shown in Eq. 4.8, where g_x^1, g_y^1, g_x^2 and g_y^2 are the x and y gradient fields for the two involved images, $\hat{g}_x$ and $\hat{g}_y$ are the x and y gradient fields after the blending and μ is the smoothing transition function. Concretely, a 3rd order Hermite function is applied. The advantage of performing the weighted average in the gradient domain is the automatic compensation for different exposures between neighboring images when the luminance image is integrated from the gradients as a final step.

$$g_x(x, y) = \mu \cdot g_x^1(x, y) + (1 - \mu) \cdot g_x^2(x, y)$$
$$g_y(x, y) = \mu \cdot g_y^1(x, y) + (1 - \mu) \cdot g_y^2(x, y)$$

$$(4.8)$$

4.5 Luminance Recovery from Gradient Fields

After independently processing each overlapping strip region around the seams, the resulting patches need to be unified into a single, larger image. Each patch processed should be updated on the final photo-mosaic image, while information which belongs to regions without overlap should be recovered from the corresponding original images.

Once the final gradient domain photo-mosaic has been composed after the "strip-blending", a non-integrable or inconsistent gradient field is obtained. In order to recover the luminance values from the gradient fields, a multigrid Poisson solver [17] is used.

4.6 Tone Mapping

The solution provided by the gradient solver is defined up to a free additive term on the recovered intensity value. Consequently, a mapping algorithm such as Minimum Information Loss [18] should be applied to determine this factor. The main goal of the mapping algorithm is to appropriately manipulate the dynamic range of the computed image in order to make it fit into the limited range of a display device while keeping the maximum amount of detail information.

4.7 Giga-Mosaic Unification

The photo-mosaicing pipeline described is currently implemented in Matlab™, using Matlab EXecutable (MEX) files and parallel computing when possible. This allows the efficient blending of photo-mosaics up to 60 Mpixels in a standard personal computer with 4 GB of RAM in less than 5 min. Nevertheless, this mosaic size (i.e. <0.1 Gpixels) is small at the gigapixel scale in which this work is interested, and a solution should be used to reach the desired 5–15 Gpixels required to process the currently available data sets.

The amount of RAM may become a limitation when dealing with gigapixel images, especially if the images have more than 8 bpp (e.g. 16-bpp grayscale images or 24/48-bpp color images). The strategy proposed to reduce the computer requirements consists of decomposing the problem into sub-problems (i.e. rectangular *tiles*) in order to sequentially solve them and finally unify them into the final mosaic image.

The price of this decomposition is the need of a second level of blending of the tiles. This one is similar to the "strip-blending" presented in Sect. 4.4.2 applied to the optimal seams, but is performed in the intensity domain. This second level of blending is performed only in the intensity domain for computational reasons. When compared with gradient domain operations, intensity blending is inexpensive and can deal with large amounts of data. Furthermore, this method does not lead to loss of quality due to the particular conditions in which it is applied. There are two reasons for the need of a blending step between neighboring tiles. The first is the different free factor of every tile after the luminance recovery using the Poisson solver since this factor is multiplicative when working with *log I* values. The second is the nature of the Poisson solver which spreads the inconsistency of the gradient fields along the whole area recovered. After multiplying the pixel intensities of every tile with the corresponding constant factor, a *tile-overlap* intensity blending has to be performed. This kind of blending will compensate the gradient differences of overlapping tiles coming from different Poisson solutions. The decomposition necessarily differs from the theoretically exact Poisson solution, given that the errors due to gradient inconsistencies will be differently spread by the solver in both cases. Nevertheless, these differences are negligible in practice.

Although the *tile-level* pipeline described above is straightforward, its technical implementation deserves further clarifications owing to the need to manage available computational resources with such large problems (i.e. gigapixel photo-mosaics).

The rectangular "canvas" of the full photo-mosaic is divided into a regular grid of overlapping *tiles* in order to process it using an *out-of-core* algorithm [19]. The size of the *tiles* depends on the available RAM. For time efficiency, the space required to store a single tile and a full *global-strip* (i.e. a row of tiles) is allocated to memory, avoiding an excessive amount of slow hard drive sequential accesses.

A weighted average smoothing in the intensity domain is used to join neighboring *tiles* in a given rectangular overlapping region. In our experiments, the size of the overlapping regions varied between 15 and 25 % of the *tile* size depending on the initial spatial image arrangement. Once a *tile* has been processed, it is stored in the current *global-strip*, performing a blending with the previously processed one (when available). When a single *global-strip* has been processed, it is stored in the hard drive to save RAM space and the same procedure is repeated on the next one. The strategy used to blend two neighboring *tiles* is also used to blend two neighboring *global-strips*. Performing the blending in this structured way avoids the problem of simultaneously fusing more than two images of a given region, which may make the computation of a transition function of the overlapping areas more complex. Figure 4.7 shows the giga-mosaic unification strategy described above.

Fig. 4.7 Tiling scheme for the gga-photo-mosaic blending. Each *tile* is processed as an independent photo-mosaic and blended with previously processed neighboring ones in a given *global-strip* (i.e. a row of blended tiles), using a weighted average in the luminance domain. Next, each two neighboring *rows* are blended using the same approach. The Giga-photo-mosaic is the result of joining all the *global-strips*

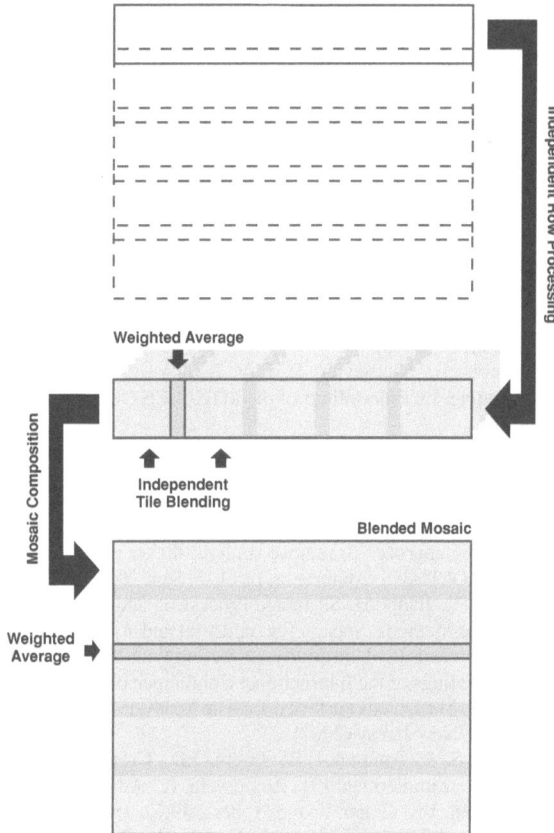

4.8 Conclusions

The main underwater imaging issues affecting underwater photo-mosaicing have been treated by the approach presented. For each one of the specific underwater imagery problems, a working solution has been presented and a new processing pipeline has been defined. In the preprocessing stage, an adaptive non-uniform illumination compensation based on a sliding window on the depth sorted image sequences has been proposed. This function allows not only giving an homogeneous appearance to a sequence of images, but also enhances hidden details in the case of high dynamic range images. Concerning exposure variations, the blending strategy based on the image gradients allows the avoidance of dealing with this problem, inasmuch as gradient methods are not sensitive to exposure variations. In the context of gradient domain methods, a novel hybrid luminance and gradient based graph-cut strategy has been presented, allowing the avoidance of problems concerning exposure variations and moving objects in the scene. Light attenuation and forward scattering lead to loss of contrast and poor detail in the images. In order to solve this issue, an adaptive image enhancement, based on the selection of the highest quality image in a given surrounding as the image sharpness reference, has been presented. The approach allows giving an homogeneous appearance to the images involved, and to enhance, up to a reasonable level, the sharpness of the original images. Finally, and aiming to efficiently generate high-resolution large-scale mosaics, a method to subdivide the mosaic into smaller and easily processable tiles has been presented.

References

1. Goldstein, E.B.: Sensation and perception. In: PSY 385 Perception Series. Cengage Learning, Stamford (2010)
2. Garcia, R., Nicosevici, T., Cufi, X.: On the way to solve lighting problems in underwater imaging. In: Proceedings of the MTS/IEEE OCEANS Conference, vol. 2, pp. 1018–1024, Oct 2002
3. Capel, D.: Image Mosaicing and Super-Resolution. Springer, Berlin (2004)
4. Rzhanov, Y., Gu, F.: Enhancement of underwater videomosaics for post-processing. In: Proceedings of the MTS/IEEE OCEANS Conference, pp. 1–6, Oct 2007
5. Gracias, N., Negahdaripour, S., Neumann, L., Prados, R., Garcia, R.: A motion compensated filtering approach to remove sunlight flicker in shallow water images. In: Proceedings of the IEEE OCEANS Conference, pp. 1–7, Sept 2008
6. Chan, T., Jianhong, S.: Image Processing and Analysis: Variational, PDE, Wavelet, and Stochastic Methods. Society for Industrial and Applied Mathematics, Philadelphia (2005)
7. Guillemaud, R.: Uniformity correction with homomorphic filtering on region of interest. In: Proceedings of the International Conference on Image Processing (ICIP), pp. 872–875 (1998)
8. Ebner, M.: Color constancy. In: The Wiley-IS&T Series in Imaging Science and Technology. Wiley, New Jeresy (2007)
9. Pizer, S.M., Amburn, E.P., Austin, J.D., Cromartie, R., Geselowitz, A., Greer, T., Romeny, B.T.H., Zimmerman, J.B., Zuiderveld, K.: Adaptive histogram equalization and its variations. Comput. Vis. Graph. Image Process. **39**(3), 355–368 (1987)
10. Reinhard, E., Adhikhmin, M., Gooch, B., Shirley, P.: Color transfer between images. IEEE Comput. Graph. Appl. **21**(5), 34–41 (2001)
11. Harris, C., Stephens, M.: A combined corner and edge detector. In: Proceedings of the Alvey Vision Conference, Manchester, UK, pp. 189–192, Aug 1988
12. Lowe, D.: Distinctive image features from scale-invariant keypoints. Int. J. Comput. Vis. **60**(2), 91–110 (2004)
13. Bay, H., Tuytelaars, T., Van Gool, L.: SURF: speeded up robust features. In: European Conference on Computer Vision, pp. 404–417 (2006)
14. Ferrer, J., Elibol, A., Delaunoy, O., Gracias, N., Garcia, R.: Large-area photo-mosaics using global alignment and navigation data. In: Proceedings of the IEEE OCEANS Conference, pp. 1–9, Oct 2007
15. Elibol, A., Garcia, R., Delaunoy, O., Gracias, N.: A new global alignment method for feature based image mosaicing. In: Proceedings of the International Symposium on Advances in Visual Computing (ISVC), Part II, pp. 257–266. Springer, Berlin, Heidelberg (2008)
16. Gracias, N., Mahoor, M., Negahdaripour, S., Gleason, A.: Fast image blending using watersheds and graph cuts. Image Vis. Comput. **27**, 597–607 (2009)
17. Kazhdan, M., Hoppe, H.: Streaming multigrid for gradient-domain operations on large images. ACM Trans. Graph. (SIGGRAPH) **27**(3), 1–10 (2008)
18. Neumann, L., Matkovic, K., Purgathofer, W.: Automatic exposure in computer graphics based on the minimum information loss principle. In: IEEE Computer Society, Hannover, Germany, vol. 0, pp. 666–667 (1998)
19. Vitter, J.S.: External memory algorithms and data structures: dealing with massive data. ACM Comput. Surv. (CSUR) **33**(2), 209–271 (2001)

Chapter 5
Results

Abstract This chapter validates the proposed processing pipeline across several seafloor datasets, in order to evaluate its performance in different scenarios. The three first datasets belong to large-scale optical surveys of the Mid-Atlantic Ridge, and where acquired by the VICTOR-6000 ROV during three different scientific cruises over the last 8 years. These datasets are composed by thousands of grayscale images and cover hundreds of square meters. These datasets allow demonstrating the suitability of the proposed solution when facing large datasets of images affected by the previously described underwater phenomena, and consequently showing constantly varying appearances. The pipeline is also used to process a shipwreck dataset acquired by the Girona 500 AUV, in order to test its performance when facing high-resolution color images. The relevance of the proposed blending pipeline for scientific purposes is demonstrated, with applications such as change detection and monitoring of interest areas over time. Finally, the obtained results are summarized and evaluated.

Keywords High-quality photo-mosaic · Large-scale underwater surveys · Temporal variations

The algorithms making up the proposed processing pipeline have been conceived to address several specific underwater imagery problems. These problems are present in the various underwater sequences used to test the performance of the approach. Some of the main sequence properties are the large number of images (from hundreds to tens or hundreds of thousands), the image acquisition using artificial light and at frequently changing depths, the presence of particles in suspension and moving objects (mainly fishes and algae, but also warm water outflow) and the significant relief changes inducing parallax effects.

In the following sections, the datasets used for testing purposes are described and their main properties are pointed out. The problems present in each are listed as well, and the performance of the approach developed is evaluated. Given the nature of the datasets, a comparison of the results obtained with a known groundtruth is

R. Prados et al., *Image Blending Techniques and their Application in Underwater Mosaicing*, SpringerBriefs in Computer Science, DOI: 10.1007/978-3-319-05558-9_5, © The Author(s) 2014

not feasible. Consequently, a numerical evaluation of the results cannot be provided. Therefore, the goodness of the results is measured based on several aspects such as the consistency of the appearance of the mosaic obtained over the area covered, the avoidance of double contours or structures and the ability to keep the most informative data in those areas where images of different quality overlap. Furthermore, comparisons with some of the most widely used [1] and best performing [2] state-of-the-art methods are also presented.

5.1 Testing Datasets

The developed processing pipeline has been tested in two different kinds of datasets. Firstly, the algorithms have been applied to several extensive image surveys intended to characterize and monitor the evolution of hydrothermal sites along the Mid-Atlantic Ridge. Secondly, a very-high resolution color image dataset belonging to the seventeenth century LaLune shipwreck (Toulon, France) prospection has been also used, to verify the performance of the proposed approach when dealing with color images.

Hydrothermal activity along mid-ocean ridges accounts for ~30 % of the Earth's oceanic heat flux, a third of which takes place on or near the mid-ocean ridge axes [3, 4]. As explained in [5], photo-mosaics of large seafloor areas in repeated surveys can be used for temporal studies of active processes. Imagery provides constraints of temporal variability at two time-scales. On the one hand, based upon changes in individual outflow features identified in mosaics acquired in different years, it is possible to monitor the evolution of diffuse outflow throughout the vent field over time. On the other hand, photo-mosaics reveal broad patches of seafloor which can be interpreted as fossil outflow zones owing to their association with extinct chimneys and hydrothermal deposits. The structures are not recognizable from video imagery alone, or from photomosaics with less efficient removal of artifacts (e.g. ghosts and seams). Repeated image surveys with adequate processing can be routinely performed to characterize and study the temporal variability of a broad range of sites hosting active processes (e.g., cold seeps, hydrothermal fields, gas outflows, etc.), opening the possibility of better understanding the dynamics of fluid flows in the sub-seafloor as well as quantification of fluxes, among many active processes occurring at the seafloor.

Over the last 14 years, numerous surveys of the Lucky Strike hydrothermal field on the Mid-Atlantic Ridge south of the Azores Islands have been performed. During this period, the three major vent fields, Menez Gwen (average depth 850 m), Lucky Strike (average depth 1650 m) and Rainbow (average depth 2300 m) were discovered along the Mid-Atlantic Ridge and extensively studied from the biological and geological points of view. Lucky Strike mosaics, generated from >56,000 images acquired in 1996, 2006, 2008 and 2009, reveal the distribution and type of diffuse outflow throughout the field and their association with high-temperature hydrothermal vents. The 1996 and 2008 surveys were the most extensive for the Lucky Strike field giving

Fig. 5.1 ROV VICTOR 6000 (IFREMER, France), with the geophysical survey module, being deployed at the Lucky Strike area along the Mid-Atlantic Ridge, during one of the surveys carried out as a part of the MOMAR08-Leg1 Cruise (CNRS/IFREMER, France). Copyright: CNRS/IFREMER

a detailed characterization of actively venting areas, including the spatial distribution of outflow zones, their type, as well as their relationship to substrate and structure [5]. Nevertheless, the 1996 survey, which optical imagery was acquired by a different camera than the subsequent ones, is not taken into account hereinafter, given the aggressive level of local filtering that suffer all its images.

The datasets presented below were collected by the Victor-6000 ROV [6] (Fig. 5.1) deployed by the oceanographic vessel *Pourquoi pas?* from IFREMER, during the various MoMAR (Monitoring the Mid-Atlantic Ridge) cruises (CNRS/IFREMER, France). The acquisition was performed with a grayscale, high sensibility camera system (OTUS) installed in the geophysical mapping payload (Module Route) at an altitude of ~5–10 m from the seafloor. The OTUS camera features a Thompson MPP CCD grayscale sensor with a resolution of 1 Mpixel and 14 bits per pixel. The frequency of the acquisition was 1 image every 5 s and the optical data was stored in TIFF format. The payload also included 4 Flashes (1,200 J), a RESON Seabat 7125 multi-beam echo sounder and a SIMRAD EK60 echo sounder altimeter. The onboard navigation system also included an RDI Doppler Velocity Log (DVL), an iXSEA OCTANS fiber-optic gyrocompass and a Paroscientific depth sensor. A calibration to obtain the intrinsic parameters of the OTUS camera was performed based on the Bathyluck 2009 images, with a calibration pattern deployed at the seafloor, and then used for the 2006, 2008 and 2009 mosaics.

5.2 MoMARETO'06 (Dataset #1)

The dataset consists of 4,628 grayscale images of 1 Mpixel with 14 bits of color depth and stored in 16-bit TIFF format. During the cruise the three major vent fields (Menez Gwen, Lucky Strike and Rainbow) were visited. The images suffer from

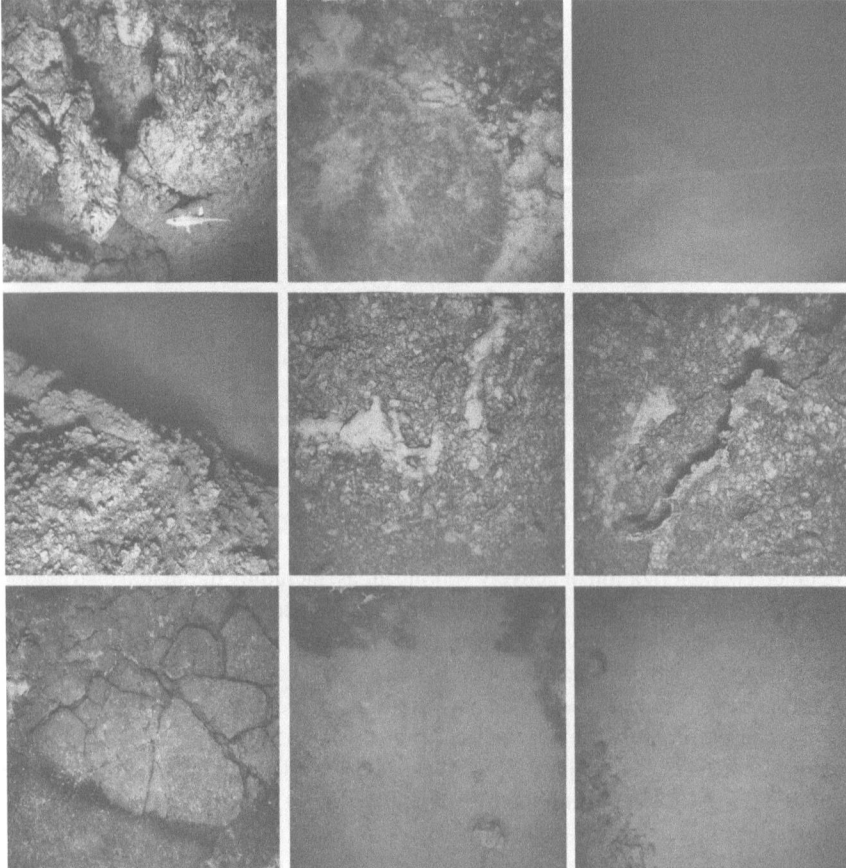

Fig. 5.2 Subset of 9 images belonging to the MoMARETO'06 (IFREMER, France) cruise dataset. The dataset consists of 4,628 grayscale images of 1 Mpixel with 14 bits of color depth and stored in 16-bit TIFF format. During the cruise the three major vent fields (Menez Gwen, Lucky Strike and Rainbow) were visited

non-uniform illumination, depict frequent slopes that emphasize the effects of light attenuation, and present sporadic moving fishes (see Fig. 5.2). Despite the fact that the area covered by the exploration was extensive (larger than 1 km^2), the acquisition was very sparse, and rarely more than two parallel transects overlap.

The resulting blended mosaic for the Lucky Strike hydrothermal field was rendered with a resolution of 10 mm/pixel, resulting in an image of 117,836 × 85,924 pixels stored using 16-bit per pixel (≈ 9.4 GPixels), i.e. 18.8 GBytes of RAW data (see Fig. 5.3). The benefits of the blended version of the mosaic when compared with the non-blended one are evident (see Fig. 5.4). Blending does not only allow obtaining a more visually agreeable, continuous and consistent representation of the seafloor, but also emphasizes several structures and details in the scene. Thanks to

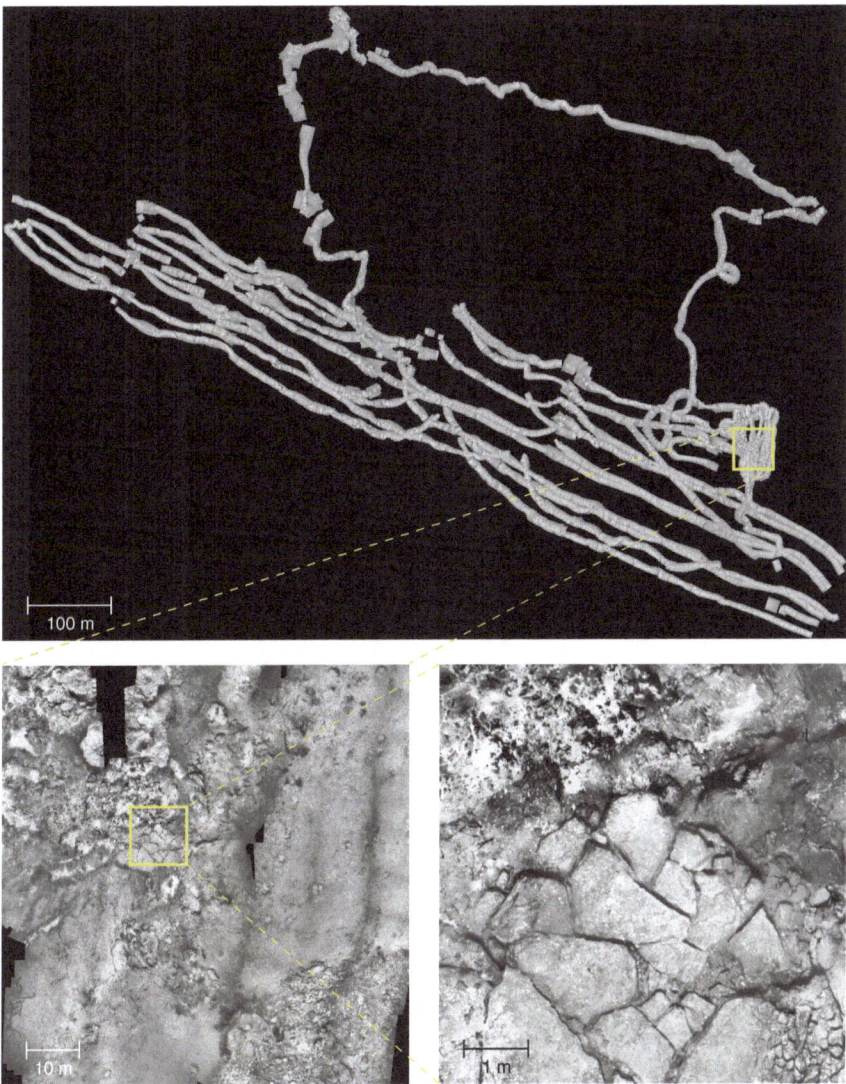

Fig. 5.3 MoMARETO'06 blended full mosaic at the Lucky Strike vent field and detailed region. The mosaic contains 4,628 grayscale images of 1 Mpixel with 14 bit of color depth and has been rendered at 10 mm/pixel, resulting in an image of 117,836 × 85,924 pixels

the prioritization carried out by both the image discarding mechanism and the image weighting performed during the pixel level graph cut, the images with higher quality also have a higher contribution to the final rendering than the lower and less informative ones.

From a cognitive point of view, the proposed pipeline emphasizes fine details, in contrast to other state-of-the-art methods, such as [2], as can be seen in Fig. 5.5. In this

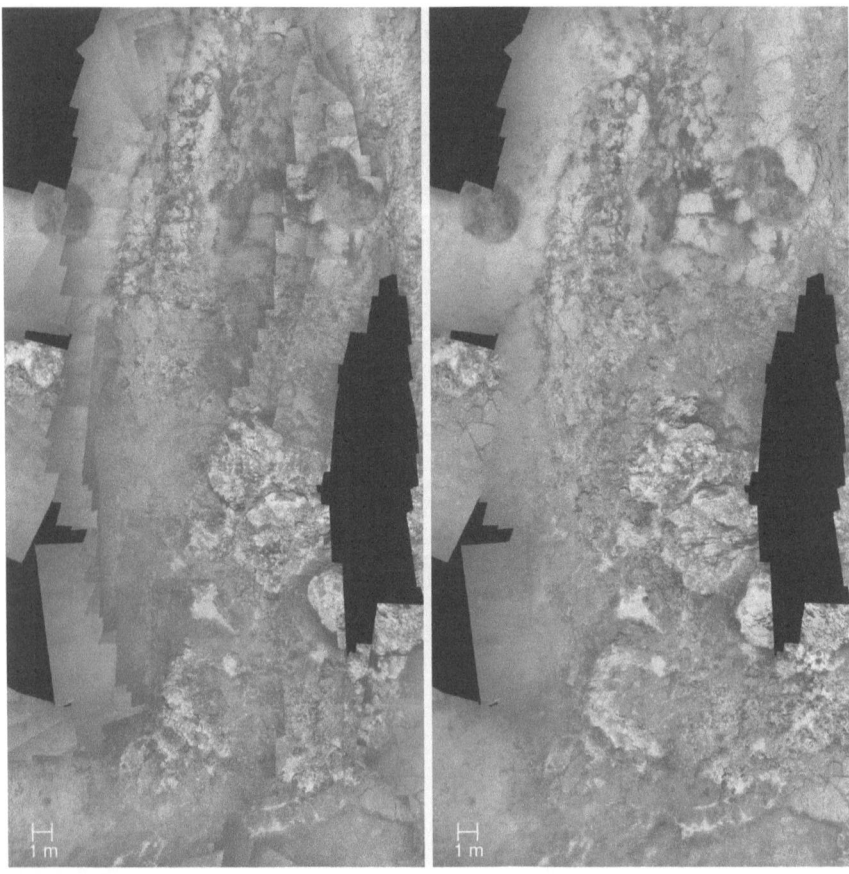

Fig. 5.4 MoMARETO'06 detailed region 1. *The left image* shows the mosaic region rendered by drawing one image on top of the previous one (*Last In* approach). The image boundaries are obvious, especially due to their darker corners. Moreover, the global appearance of the photo-mosaic is not consistent, presenting regions with more contrast than others. The *right image* shows the mosaic region rendered when using the proposed approach. In this case, the image boundaries are not visible and the appearance is consistent throughout the whole area. Furthermore, some details obfuscated in the *Last In* rendering show clearly in the blended version, thanks to the quality based image selection mechanism

case, although both methods obtain very convincing results, the proposed approach helps the interpretation task by keeping small structures visible and selecting the most contrastful view of the scene's elements, better defining small details on the seafloor.

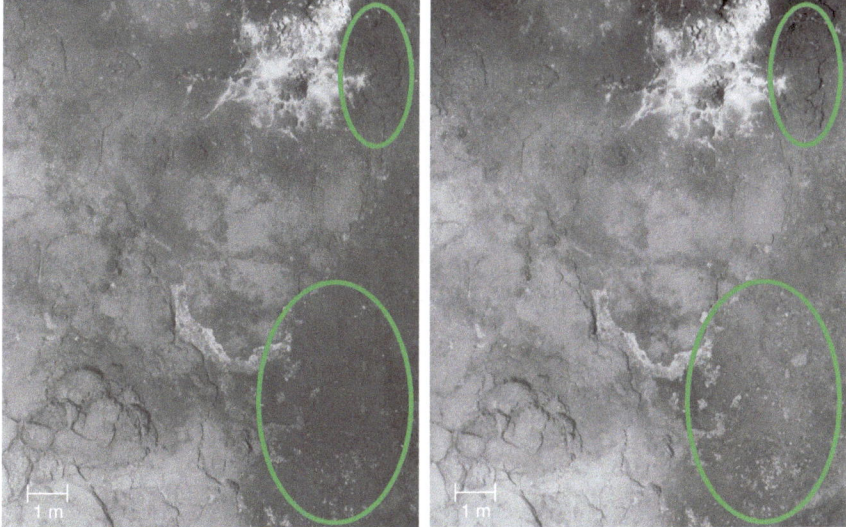

Fig. 5.5 MoMARETO'06 detailed region 2. The *left image* shows the result obtained by Szeliski's method [2] and the *right image* shows the result of the proposed pipeline. Despite both being very convincing, it can be seen that the quality based image selection mechanism of the proposed method has allowed highlighting some of the details in the murky regions as well as sharply defining the features with higher contrast in the rest of the image

5.3 MoMAR'08 (Dataset #2)

The dataset consists of 21,635 images of 1 Mpixel with 14 bits of color depth and stored in 16-bit TIFF format. A 3-day survey of the Lucky Strike hydrothermal field was performed in order to acquire all the optical data. As with dataset #1, the images suffer from non-uniform illumination, depict frequent slopes that emphasize the effects of light attenuation, and present sporadic moving fishes (see Fig. 5.6). Nevertheless, in this case, the density of the acquisition in the interest area (larger than 1km^2) is considerably high, presenting common overlaps between two or more parallel transects.

The resulting blended mosaic was rendered with a resolution of 10 mm/pixel, resulting in an image of 78,651 × 62,722 pixels stored using 16 bits per pixel (≈ 4.6) GPixels, i.e. 9.2 GBytes of RAW data (see Fig. 5.7). As in dataset #1, the blended version of the mosaic shows a consistent appearance throughout the whole area surveyed. When compared with state-of-the-art methods, the proposed approach shows several advantages. On the one hand, it hides any visible seams when the appearance of neighboring images is significantly different, which is the common

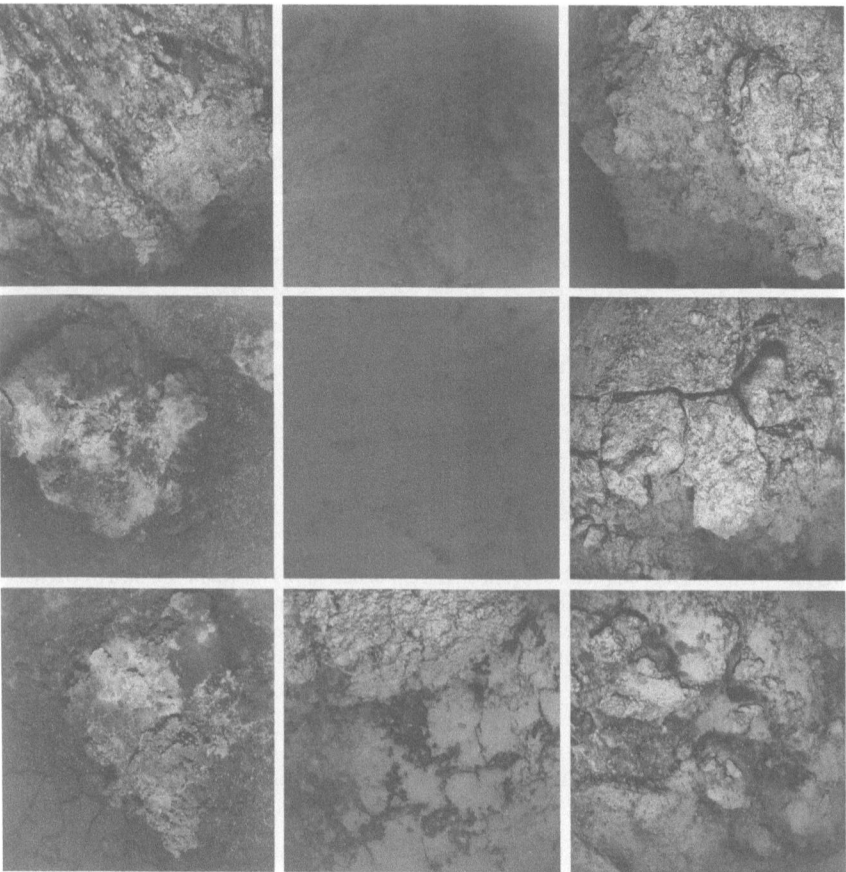

Fig. 5.6 Subset of 9 images belonging to the MoMAR'08 (CNRS/IFREMER, France) cruise dataset. The dataset consists of 21,635 grayscale images of 1 Mpixel with 14 bits of color depth and stored in 16-bit TIFF format

case when images acquired at different distances from the seafloor are combined. In that case, methods based on setting the gradient values around the optimal seam boundary to zero [7] lead to clearly noticeable seams and result in a non-continuous image (see Fig. 5.8-left). On the other hand, the presented pipeline avoids ghosting and double contouring effects when image registration or parallax happen, as opposed to some transition smoothing methods such as a weighted average in the gradient domain performed on all the available overlapping pixels [8] (see Fig. 5.8-center).

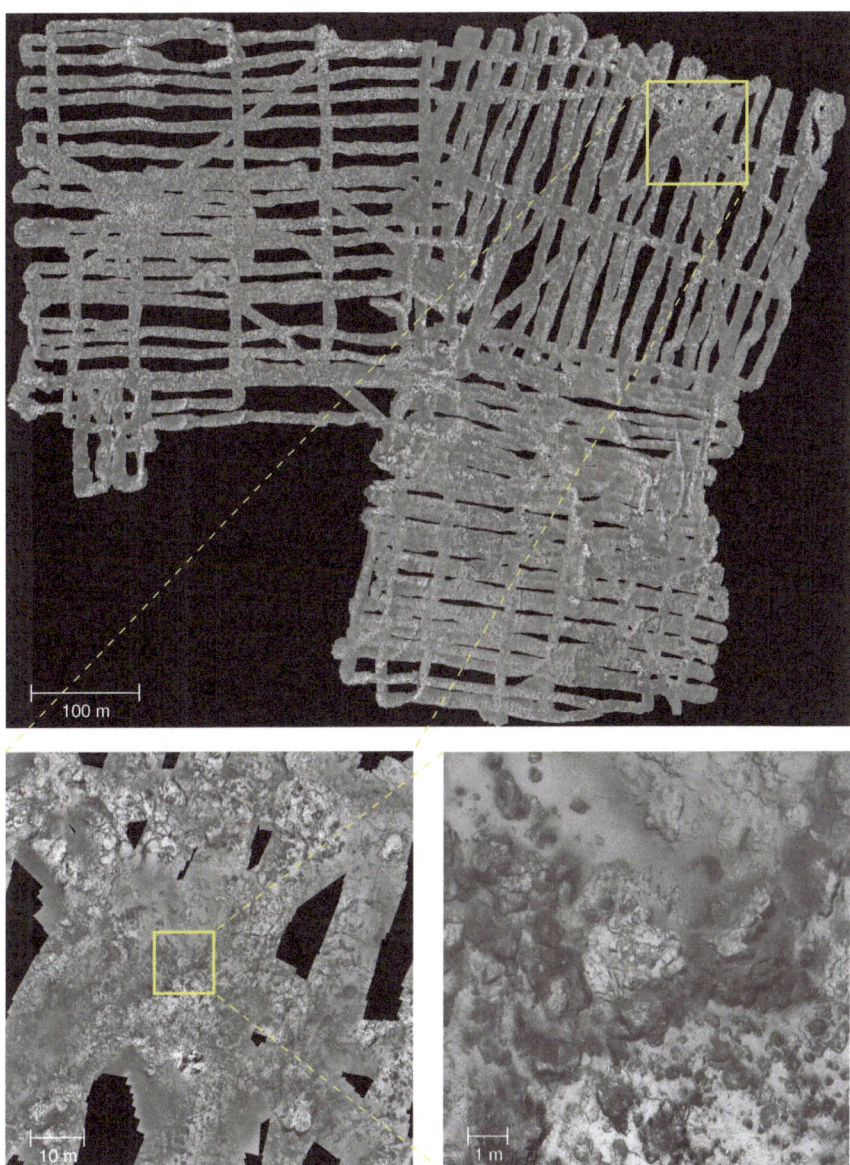

Fig. 5.7 MoMAR'08 blended full mosaic and detailed region. The mosaic contains 21,635 grayscale images of 1Mpixel with 14 bits of color depth and has been rendered at 10 mm/pixel, resulting in an image of $78,651 \times 62,722$ pixels

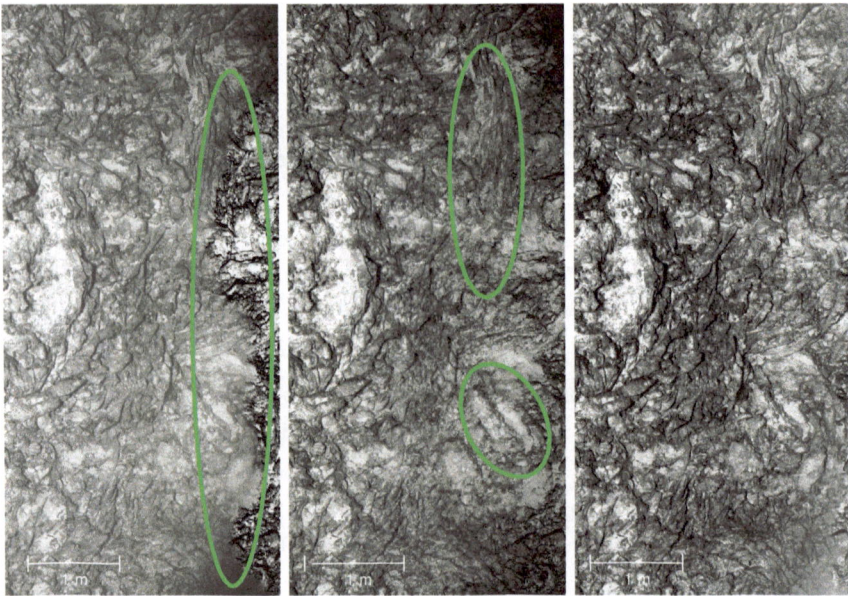

Fig. 5.8 MoMAR'08 detailed region 1. Detail of a given overlapping region blended with three different gradient approaches. *Left* shows the result of setting the gradient values around the optimal seam boundary at zero [7] in order to enforce continuity through the joint. *Center* shows the result of a weighted average gradient blending performed on all the available overlapping pixels [8]. *Right* shows the result of the proposed approach, which only performs a gradient blending on a narrow region around the optimal computed seam. The transition is sufficiently smooth to provide a sensation of consistency in the image while avoiding ghosting and double contours in the overlapping areas

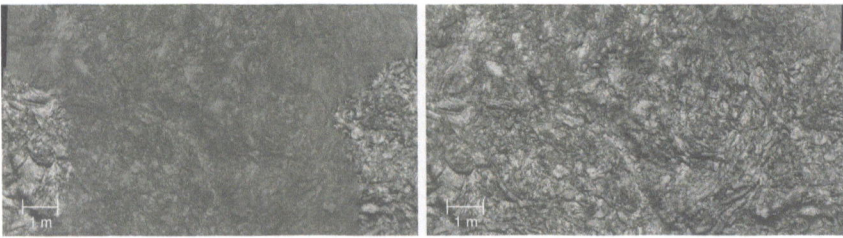

Fig. 5.9 MoMAR'08 detailed region 2. *Left* Detail of an underwater photo-mosaic region generated with Szeliski's method [2] (direct result of Microsoft ICE software) without automatic image enhancement. *Right* the result obtained by our approach with adaptive contrast enhancement. The global appearance of the image is uniform and the central part of the photo-mosaic is perceptually more informative after the contrast improvement

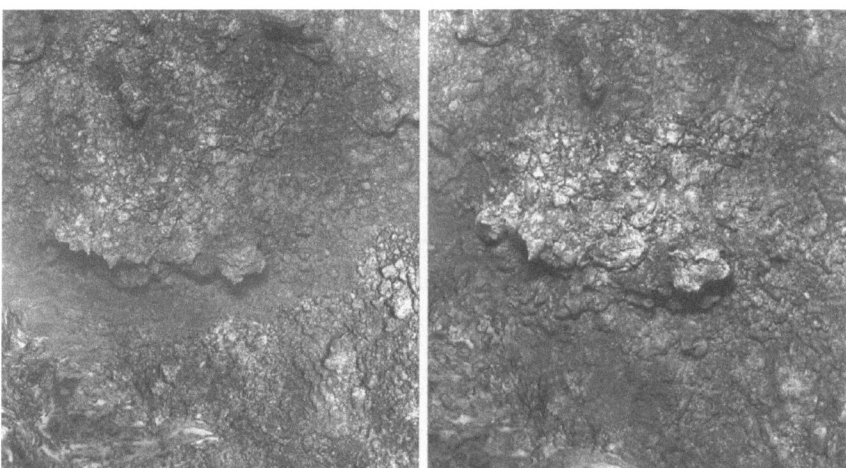

Fig. 5.10 MoMAR'08 detailed region 3. *Left* Detail of an underwater photo-mosaic region using Szeliski's method. *Right* the result obtained by our approach with contributing image selection based on a quality rank estimation. The approach proposed leads to an image richer in detail and with higher contrast

Differences in appearance beetween neighboring images are specially frequent when a given area is surveyed twice or more times in a given exploration. Concerning this problem, not only bringing a similar appearance to all the involved images but also selecting the higher quality, most informative one is a relevant task. The pipeline proposed prioritizes these images in order to use these pixels in the final mosaic. An example of the difference between the obtained results by the presented method and other state-of-the-art methods can be seen in Figs. 5.9, 5.10, 5.11.

The benefits of using blending techniques arise during the image interpretation task performed by the experts. For example, darker seafloor areas visible in the final gigamosaic are not recognizable in the original imagery (see Fig. 5.12). These structures have been interpreted as fossil hydrothermal areas, and provide a view of the evolution of the hydrothermal system over long geological periods of time. This imagery can thus be exploited to provide a comprehensive view of the different kinds of hydrothermal outflow in the Lucky Strike area, their distribution, and their relative abundances [5, 9]. The areas of active focused and diffuse hydrothermal discharge, located within the areas of fossil outflow (dark seafloor), were identified and manually marked (or digitized) in the blended photo-mosaic. Bacterial mats are reliable indicators of zones of hydrothermal outflow, primarily diffuse, with fluid temperatures as high as 150 °C locally, and thus reflect active venting. Actively venting areas can be readily identified through visual inspection of photo-mosaics.

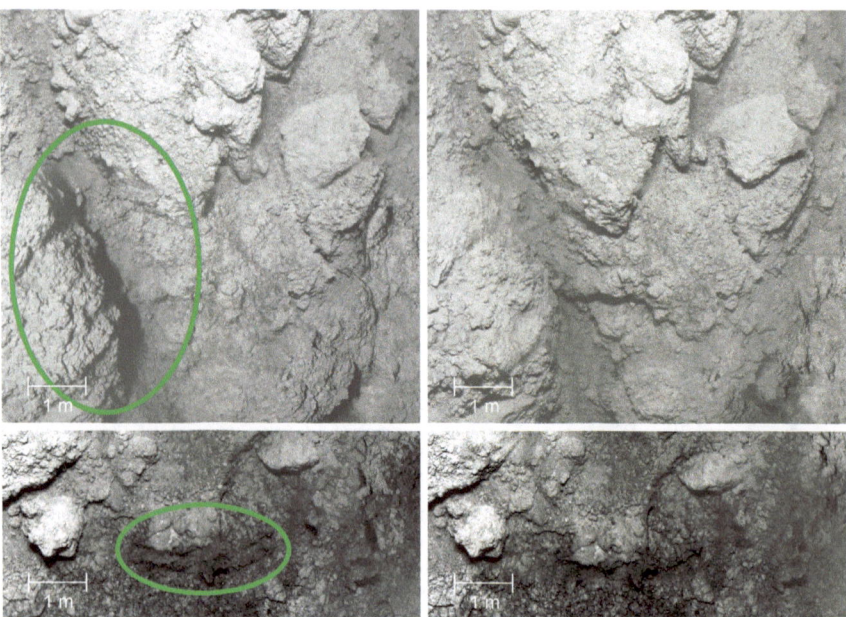

Fig. 5.11 MoMAR'08 detailed region 4. Comparison of our approach with common state-of-the-art methods in terms of graph-cut performance. *Left-top and bottom* details of an underwater mosaic region blended using an intensity based graph-cut algorithm and *Right-top and bottom* the result obtained by the proposed gradient based graph-cut strategy. *Left-top* the shadow in the top left corner region has been interpreted differently by both approaches, leading, in the case of our graph-cut *Right-top*, to an unshadowed valley. The highlighted regions in image *Left-bottom* present object doubling that has been suppressed in image *Right-bottom*. The graph-cut shows a different behavior in both cases, leading to a noticeable difference in the image contribution selection

Using dedicated image-viewing software (see [10] for details), the limits of individual features where digitized when possible, based on the full-resolution mosaic scenes (areas ~10 m wide, with a pixel resolution of 5−10 mm). Hydrothermal fluids may outflow along individual fissures or networks of fractures, around which bacterial mats and hydrothermal deposits concentrate. A kind of these fissures, called *cracks*, can also be seen in Fig. 5.15. The non-blended photo-mosaic suffers from uneven illumination in the individual images as well as a lack of contrast. Moreover, some images acquired from a far distance from the seafloor hide the information of others acquired at a closer distance. These circumstances make the identification of the interest image features difficult, whereas they are easily recognizable in the blended photo-mosaic.

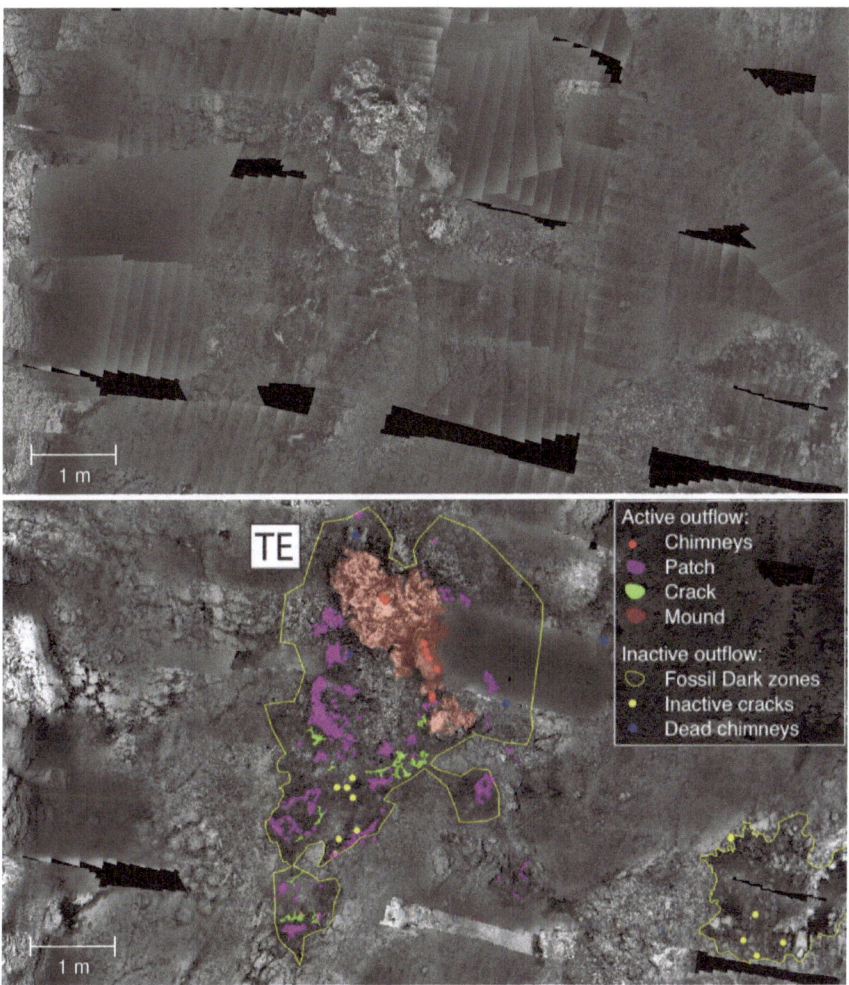

Fig. 5.12 Detail of the non-blended photo-mosaic of the southeastern part of Lucky Strike hydrothermal field (*Top*) and identified hydrothermal features, both active and inactive, in the blended photo-mosaic (*Bottom*) obtained from image mosaic interpretation and in situ observations [5]. The appearance consistency and emphasized details of the blended photo-mosaic facilitate the interpretation of the scene, and consequently the identification of all the active focused and diffuse hydrothermal discharge located within the areas of fossil outflow (*dark seafloor*). The seafloor imagery in the blended photo-mosaic corresponds to the MoMAR'08 survey, complemented in the background by the 2006 and 2009 mosaics to reduce imaging gaps. TE symbolizes *Tour Eiffel*

5.4 BATHYLUCK'09 (Dataset #3)

The dataset consists of 21,614 images also acquired with the OTUS camera (1 Mpixel resolution with 14 bits of color depth and stored in 16-bit TIFF format) over the Luck Strike area. Similar to dataset #1 and dataset #2, the images suffer from non-uniform illumination, depict frequent slopes that emphasize the effects of light attenuation, and present sporadic moving fishes (see Fig. 5.13). The density of the acquisition in the interest area (larger than $1 \, km^2$) is high in some regions but sparse in others, presenting extensive areas where overlaps between two or more parallel transects are sporadic.

The resulting blended photo-mosaic has been rendered with a resolution of 10 mm/pixel, resulting in an image of 138,502 × 232,626 pixels stored using 16

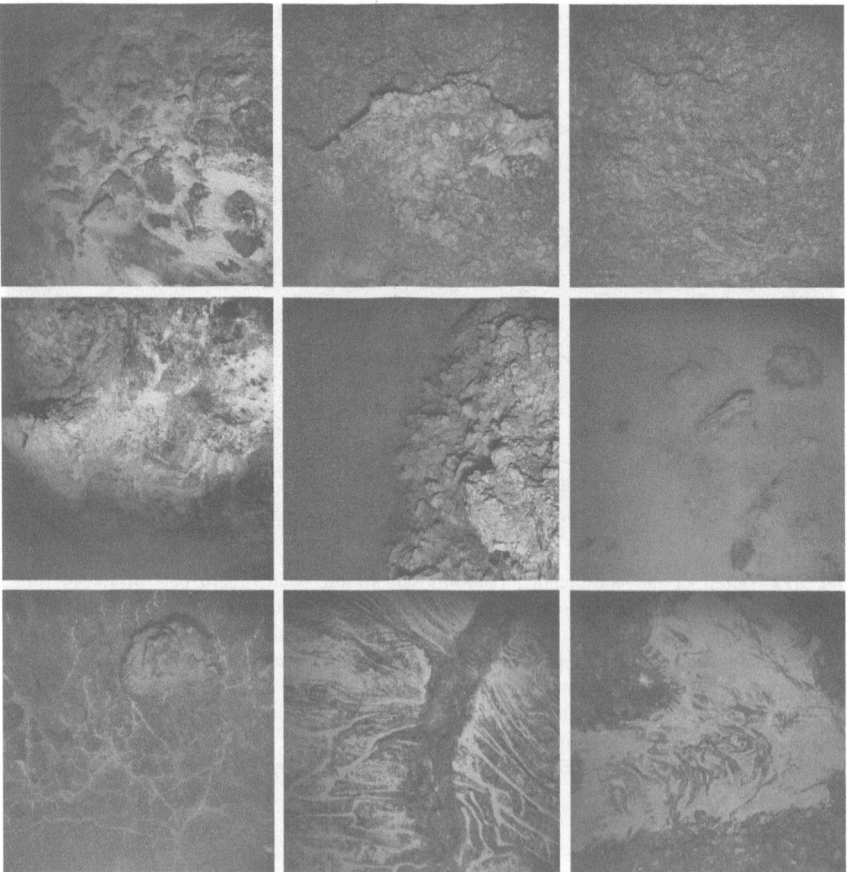

Fig. 5.13 Subset of 9 images belonging to the BATHYLUCK'09 (CNRS/IFREMER, France) cruise dataset. The dataset consists of 21,614 grayscale images of 1 Mpixel with 14 bits of color depth and stored in 16-bit TIFF format

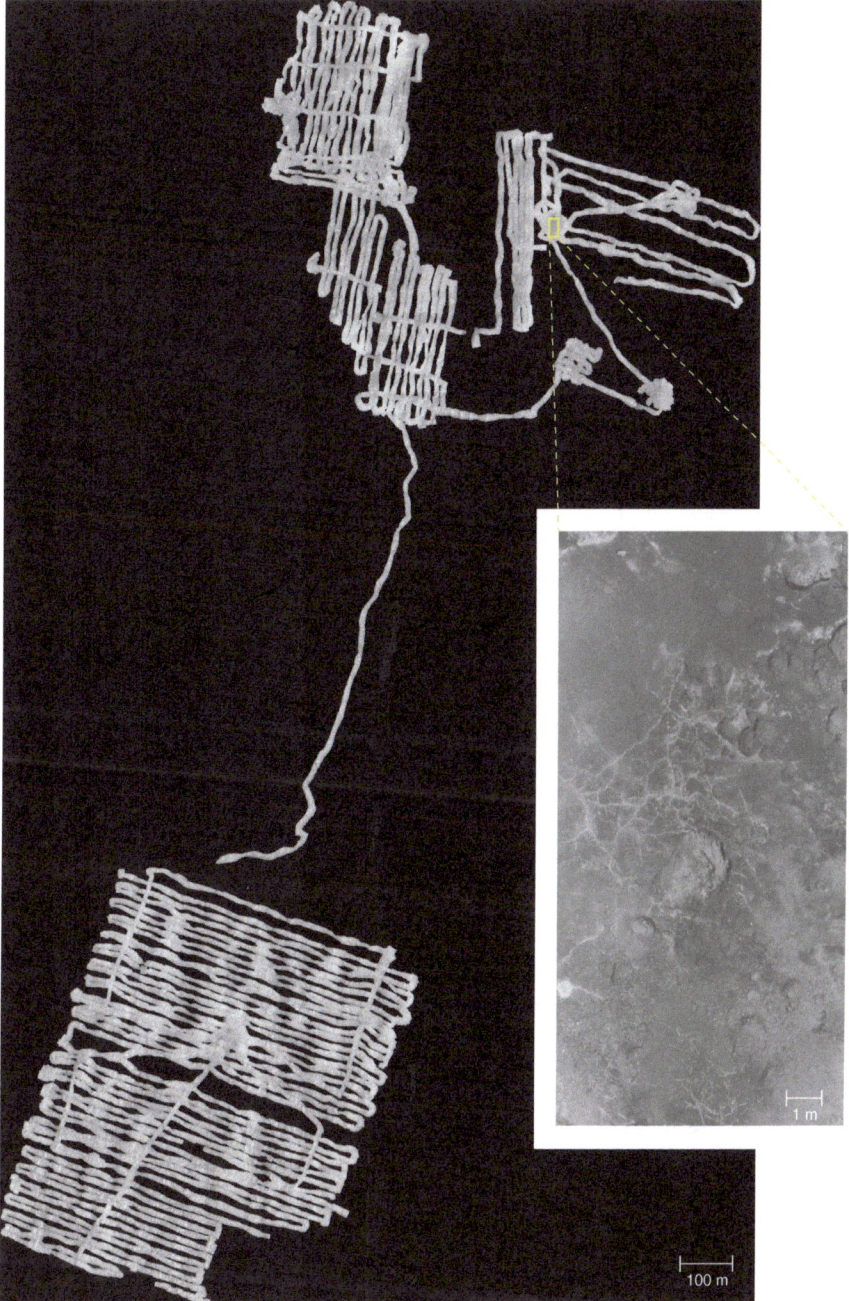

Fig. 5.14 BATHYLUCK'09 blended full mosaic and detailed region. The mosaic contains 21,614 grayscale images of 1 Mpixel with 14 bits of color depth and has been rendered at 10 mm/pixel, resulting in an image of 138,502 × 232,626 pixels

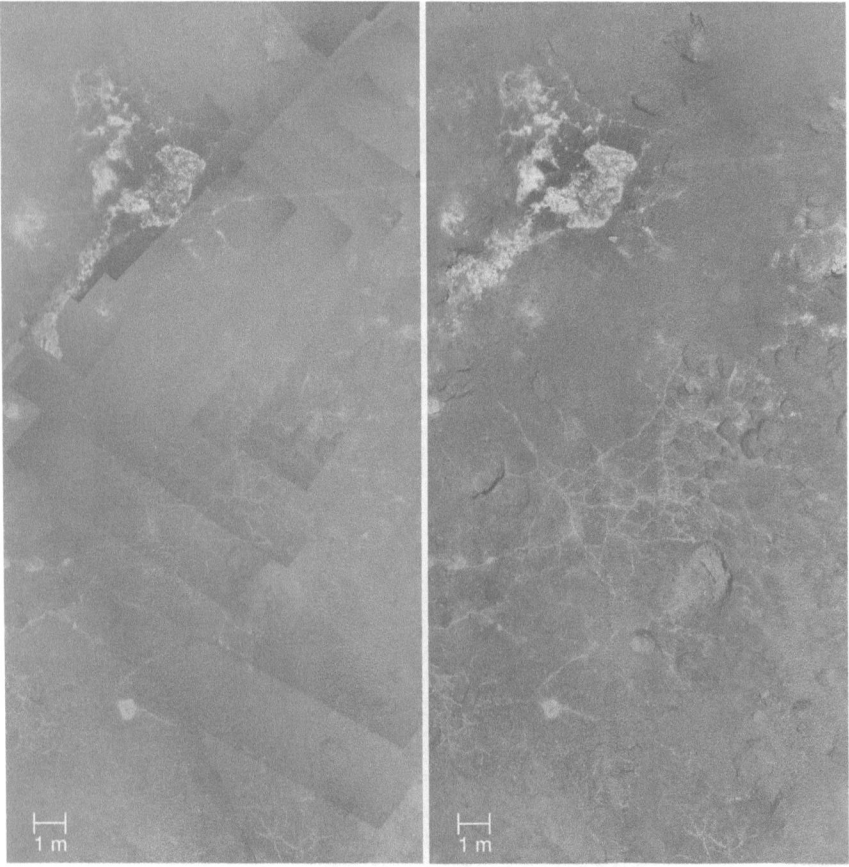

Fig. 5.15 BATHYLUCK'09 detailed region 1. The *left image* shows the mosaic region rendered by drawing one image on top of the previous one (*Last In*). The image boundaries are clearly visible, especially due to their darker corners, and the global appearance is not consistent, evidencing lack of contrast in several regions. The *right image* shows the mosaic region rendered by using the approach proposed. The image boundaries are not visible, the appearance of the image is uniform, and the fine details of the seabed structures are sharp in contrast and thereby easily distinguishable

bits per pixel (≈ 30.0 GPixels), i.e. 60.0 GBytes of RAW data (see Fig. 5.14). As in the previous cases, the blended version of the mosaic shows a consistent appearance throughout the whole area surveyed.

In the areas which have been surveyed several times (i.e. zones covered by multiple images), the image quality assessment mechanism allows selecting and emphasizing information corresponding to the seabed structures. The improvement of the results over a simple *Last In* rendering are demonstrated in Figs. 5.15, 5.16, 5.17 and 5.18.

Fig. 5.16 BATHYLUCK'09 detailed region 2. The *top image* shows the mosaic region rendered by drawing one image on top of the previous one (*Last In*). The image boundaries are clearly visible, especially due to their darker corners, and the global appearance is not consistent, evidencing lack of contrast in several regions. The *bottom image* shows the mosaic region rendered by using the approach proposed. The image boundaries are not visible, the appearance of the image is uniform, and the fine details of the seabed structures are sharp in contrast and thereby easily distinguishable

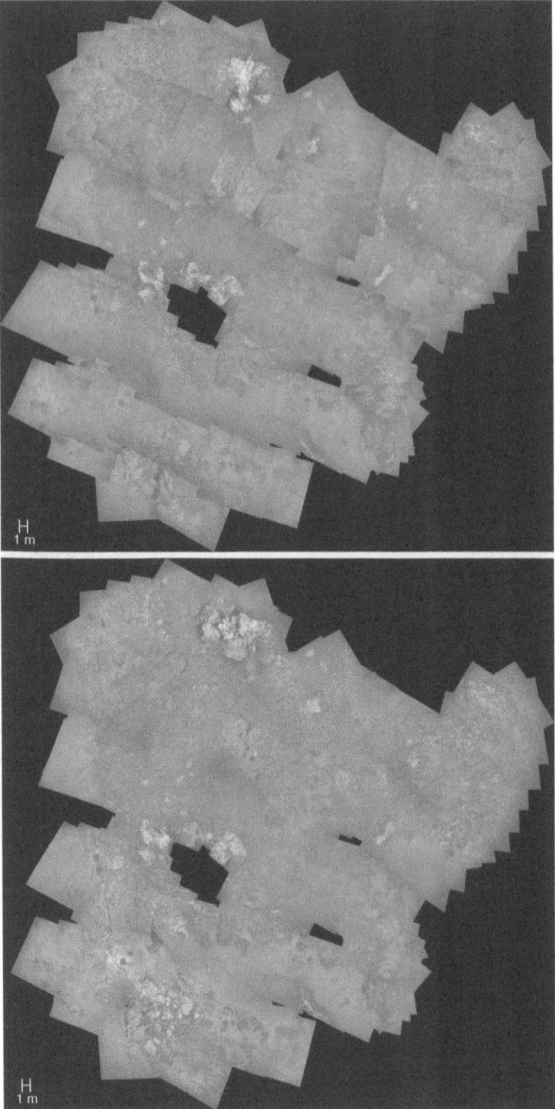

Fig. 5.17 BATHYLUCK'09 detailed region 3. The *top image* shows the mosaic region rendered by drawing one image on top of the previous one (*Last In*). The image boundaries are clearly visible, especially due to their darker corners, and the global appearance is not consistent, evidencing lack of contrast in several regions. The *bottom image* shows the mosaic region rendered by using the approach proposed. The image boundaries are not visible, the appearance of the image is uniform, and the fine details of the seabed structures are sharp in contrast and thereby easily distinguishable

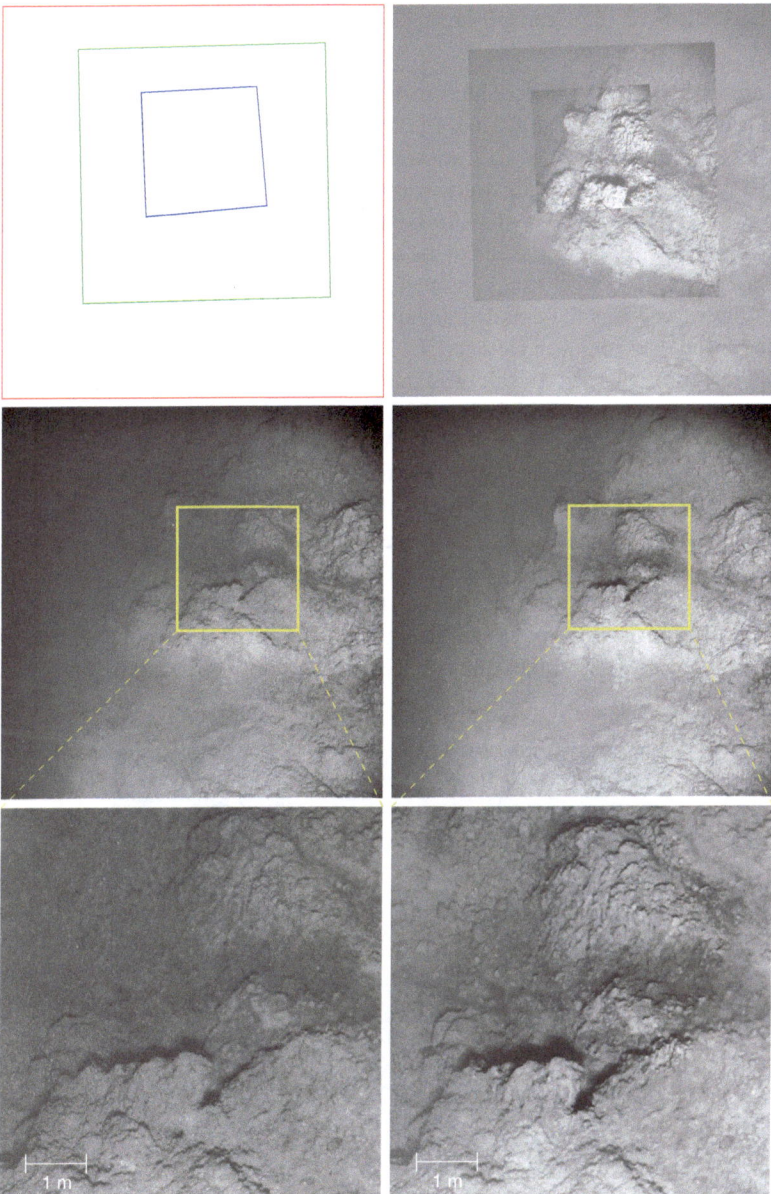

Fig. 5.18 BATHYLUCK'09 detailed region 4. *Left-top* wire-frame representation of a mosaic generated from three pictures acquired at significantly different depths. *Right-top* Last-In representation of the mosaic. The image acquired closer to the seabed is significantly sharper than the others. *Left-middle and Right-middle* photo-mosaics generated using Szeliski's method [2] and the approach proposed. *Left-bottom and Right-bottom* detail of the central part of the mosaics, where the three pictures overlap. The result of the proposed approach keeps the information from the images acquired closer to the seabed, resulting in a sharper and higher contrast representation than that obtained by the other method

5.5 LaLune'12 (Dataset #4)

The dataset consists of 845 very high-resolution color images (21 Mpixel with 8 bits of color depth and stored in 8-bit JPEG format). A survey covering the area corresponding to the shipwreck of *La Lune* was performed in August 2012 by the Girona 500 AUV (Fig. 5.19). The shipwreck was discovered by chance in 1993 by Ifremer, in the context of the ESSAUV12-2 mission, during a IFREMER Nautile submarine test dive, at a 90 m depth at the end of the roadstead of Toulon [11]. This three-masted vessel of Louis XIV's fleet sank in 1664 with a crew of more than 800 hands. The aim of the survey was the detailed documentation of the finding and scheduling of an excavation carried out in October 2012 (Fig. 5.20).

The resulting blended mosaic was rendered with a resolution of 2.5 mm/pixel, resulting in an image of 23,267 × 22,751 pixels stored using 8 bits per pixel ($\approx$ 0.5 GPixels), i.e. 18.8 GBytes of RAW data (see Fig. 5.21). The benefits of the blended version of the mosaic when compared with the non-blended one are evident (see Fig. 5.21). Blending does not only obtain a more visually agreeable, continuous and consistent representation of the seafloor, but also picks out and emphasizes several structures and details in the scene. Thanks to the prioritization carried out by both the image discarding mechanism and the image weighting performed during the pixel-level graph cut, the images with a higher quality have also a higher contribution to the final rendering than the lower and less informative ones.

Fig. 5.19 Girona 500 AUV autonomously performing an optical seafloor survey in the Mediterranean sea

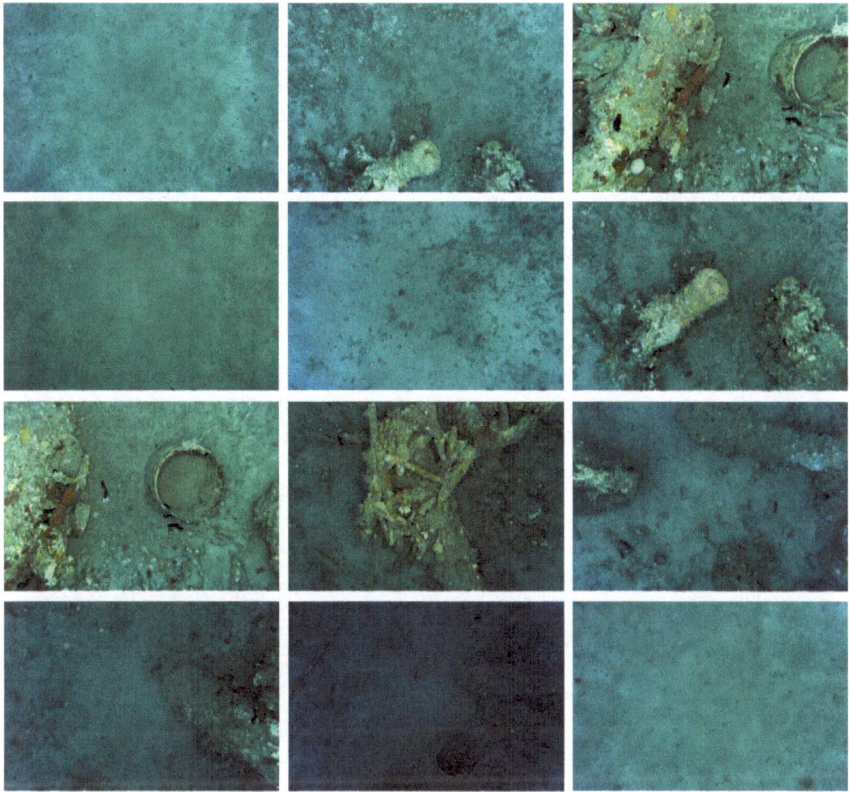

Fig. 5.20 Subset of 23 images belonging to the La Lune 2012 cruise dataset. The dataset consists of 845 grayscale images of 21 Mpixel with 8 bits of color depth and stored in 8-bit TIFF format

From the cognitive point of view, the proposed pipeline emphasizes fine details in contrast to other state-of-the-art methods, such as [2], as can be seen in Fig. 5.22. In this case, even though both approaches obtain very convincing results, the approach proposed helps the interpretation task by making small structures visible and selecting the most contrasting view of the scene elements.

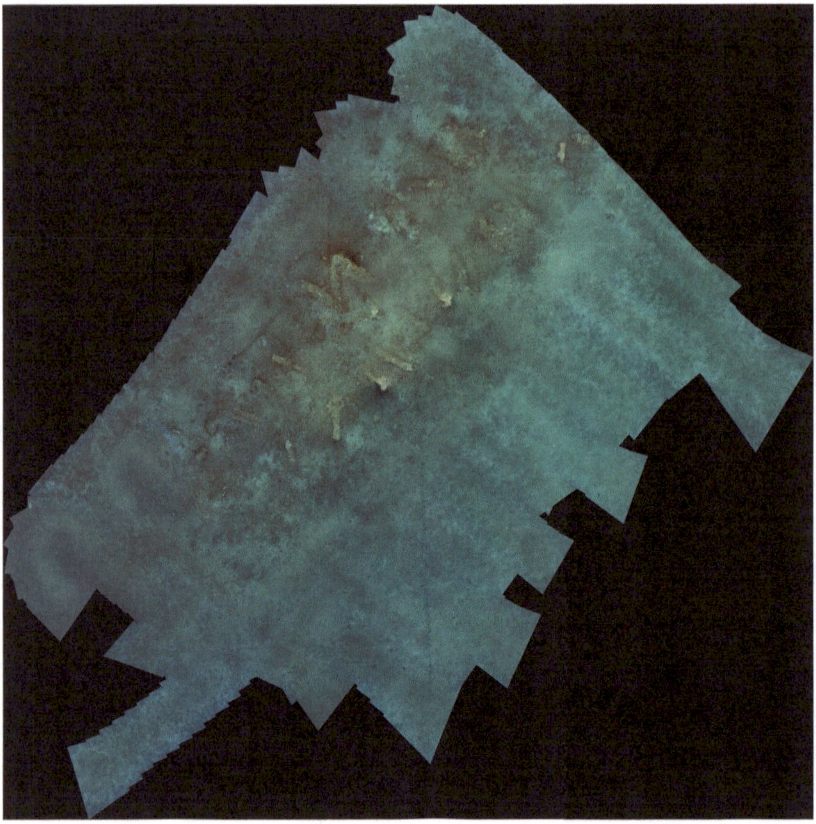

Fig. 5.21 La Lune 2012 blended full mosaic. The mosaic contains 845 color images of 21 Mpixel with 8 bits of color depth and has been rendered at 2.5 mm/pixel, resulting in an image of 23,267 × 22,751 pixels

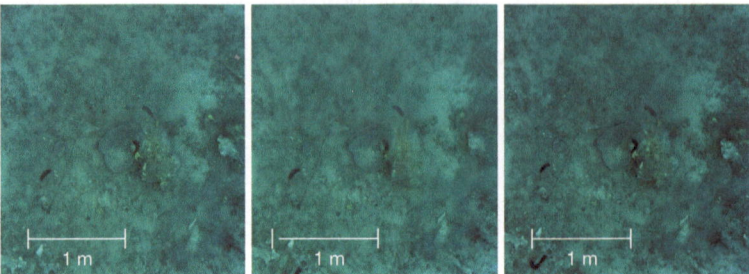

Fig. 5.22 La Lune 2012 detailed region. *Left* blended mosaic of two images obtained by the Microsoft ICE software. *Center* blended mosaic of two images using multiband blending. *Right* blended mosaic of two images obtained by the approach proposed. The result obtained by the approach proposed shows a stronger contrast and sharper appearance than that obtained by the Microsoft ICE software and the multiband blending approaches. This is due not only to the adaptive image enhancement mechanism but also to the quality based image selection in the overlapping area

5.6 Temporal Variations

As early stated, the use of blended Giga-mosaics allows an appropriate interpretation of the benthos by the scientists. These large-scale, underwater mosaics are, likewise, accurately geo-referenced. Consequently, these factors makes feasible to monitor temporal variations among repeated surveys of the same interest areas, as demonstrated in [5].

Thanks to the image quality equalization performed by the blending pipeline, the comparison of optical imagery information along the time becomes an easier task

| MoMARETO'06 | MoMAR'08 | BATHYLUCK'09 |

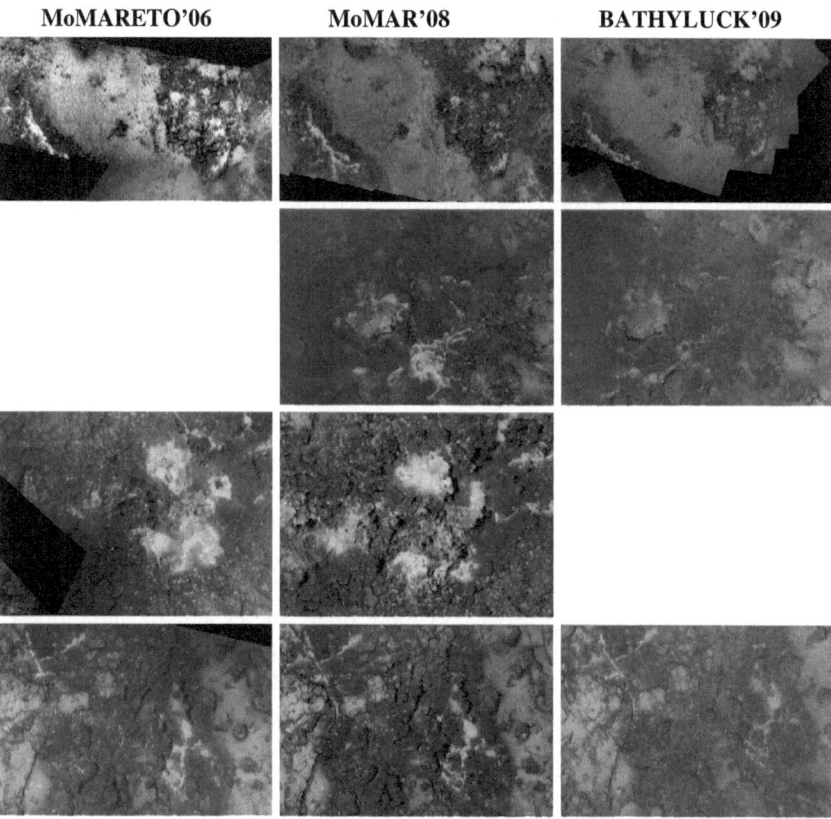

Fig. 5.23 Examples of temporal variability documented by three repeated image surveys and for four selected sites of Lucky Strike. Observed changes in the *white areas* (diffuse outflow) include an overall reduction or increase of their size, changes in their continuity and intensity, or ultimately the appearance or disappearance of active areas. *The first and second rows* represent sites with a decreasing activity along the years, *the third row* shows a site with increasing activity, and *the fourth row* depicts an stable site

than a simple study of the original, non-preprocessed images. These images typically show strongly uneven appearances between surveys, in as much as the acquisition conditions such as depth and illumination conditions may change.

An example on temporal monitoring of four interest areas, corresponding to four activity sites, and belonging to the previously presented MoMARETO'06, MoMAR'08 and BARHYLUCK'09 surveys, can bee seen in Fig. 5.23. Observed changes in the white areas (diffuse outflow) include an overall reduction or increase of their size, changes in their continuity and intensity, or ultimately the appearance or disappearance of active areas. Specifically, the first and second sites show a decreasing hydrothermal activity along the three successive surveys, the third site shows an increasing activity, and the fourth site depicts an stable area. Due to the sparseness of the acquisition, the optical imagery for some interest areas is missing.

5.7 Summary

A summary of the main properties of the processed datasets is presented in Table 5.1. Three of the four presented datasets consist of a large number of grayscale 1-Mpixel images, while the last one is composed of a smaller number but in color and with a resolution of 21 Mpixels. Consequently, all the generated mosaics are in the GPixel order, although the coverage percentage varies between datasets.

The approach proposed has demonstrated a consistent behaviour throughout all the processed sequences, in both grayscale and color images. The high quality pixel prioritization in combination with the automatic image discarding mechanism and the context based image enhancement allows improving, in most cases, the results obtained by the state-of-the-art methods. When dealing with images showing a similar appearance, i.e. acquired at similar depths and with the same illumination conditions, the improvement versus the state of the art may be small. However, when these acquisition conditions vary, which is common in underwater imagery, and specially when the same area is imaged twice or more times, the benefits of the proposed specific pipeline become obvious. In some cases, the number of images overlapping in the same area is high, although this does not happen frequently. Methods lacking from a pixel prioritization policy or an image discarding mechanism lead to image degradation and smoothing when the information from all the images is merged

Table 5.1 Testing datasets details

Name	# Images	Image size	Bit depth (bpp)	Mosaic size	Resolution (mm/pixel)	Memory* (GB)	Overlap	Cov. (%)	Hours of survey (h)
MoMARETO'06 (dataset #1)	4,628	1,024 × 1,024 × 1	14	117,836 × 85,924	10	18.8	Low	63	~34
MoMAR'08–LS (dataset #2)	21,635	1,024 × 1,024 × 1	14	78,651 × 62,722	10	9.2	High	80	~101
BATHYLUCK'09 (dataset #3)	21,614	1,024 × 1,024 × 1	14	138,502 × 232,626	10	60.0	Medium	72	~33
LaLune'12 (dataset #4)	845	5,616 × 3,744 × 3	8	23,267 × 22,751	2.5	1.5	Full	100	~1.5

* Memory usage in RAW format

in the same area. This issue is avoided by the approach proposed. Concerning the huge quantity of images in the datasets tested and the large dimensions of the final mosaics, none of the softwares used to perform the state-of-the-art tests have been able to process the whole sequence. These softwares are not intended to deal with navigation data, becoming the registration step an impossible task. For that reason, the comparisons presented, despite being representative, have been performed only in selected areas involving a reduced number of images. The improvement in terms of image understanding and interpretation are clear when comparing the blended and non-blended versions of the same mosaic.

References

1. Burt, P.J., Adelson, E.H.: A multiresolution spline with application to image mosaics. ACM Trans. Graph. (TOG) **2**(4), 217–236 (1983)
2. Szeliski, R.: Image alignment and stitching: a tutorial. Found. Trends Comput. Graph. Vision **2**(1), 1–104 (2006)
3. Stein, C.A., Stein, S.: Constraints on hydrothermal heat flux through the oceanic lithosphere from global heat flow. J Geophys. Res. **99**(B2), 3081–3095 (1994)
4. Elderfield, H., Schultz, A.: Mid-ocean ridge hydrothermal fluxes and the chemical composition of the ocean. Annu. Rev. Earth Planet. Sci. **24**, 191–224 (1996)
5. Barreyre, T., Escartin, J., Garcia, R., Cannat, M., Mittelstaedt, E., Prados, R.: Structure, temporal evolution, and heat flux estimates from a deep-sea hydrothermal field derived from seafloor image mosaics. Geochem. Geophys. Geosyst. **13**(4), 1–29 (2012)
6. Simeoni, P., Sarrazin, J., Nouze, H., Sarradin, P.M., Ondreas, H., Scalabrin, C., Sinquin, J.-M.: Victor 6000: new high resolution tools for deep sea research. module de mesures en route. In: Proceedings of the MTS/IEEE OCEANS Conference, pp. 1–6, June 2007
7. Xiang, Y., Zou, B., Li, H.: Selective color transfer with multi-source images. Pattern Recogn. Lett. **30**(7), 682–689 (2009)
8. Pérez, P., Gangnet, M., Blake, A.: Poisson image editing. ACM Trans. Graph. (SIGGRAPH) **22**(3), 313–318 (2003)
9. Mittelstaedt, E., Escartén, J., Gracias, N., Olive, J. A., Barreyre, T., Davaille, A., Cannat, M., Garcia, R.: Quantifying diffuse and discrete venting at the tour eiffel vent site, lucky strike hydrothermal field. Geochem. Geophys. Geosyst. **13** (2012)
10. Escartin, J., Garcia, R., Delaunoy, O., Ferrer, J., Gracias, N., Elibol, A., Cufi, X., Neumann, L., Fornari, D.J., Humphris, S.E., Renard, J.: Globally aligned photomosaic of the lucky strike hydrothermal vent field (Mid-Atlantic ridge, 37° 18.5'N): Release of georeferenced data, mosaic construction, and viewing software. Geochem. Geophys. Geosyst. **9** (2008)
11. Ifremer. L'épave de La Lune, vieille de 350 ans, révélée au large de Toulon. http://wwz.ifremer.fr/institut/Les-ressources-documentaires/Medias/Communiques-de-presse/L-epave-de-La-Lune-revelee. Accessed 07 Jan 2013

Chapter 6
Conclusions

Abstract This chapter summarizes the contents and contributions of this monograph. First, the need of an specific processing pipeline for large-scale underwater photo-mosaicing is pointed out. Next, the requirements of a optimal blending technique obtained from the analysis of the state-of-the-art methods and the proposed classification are detailed. Then, the contributions of the work in the different steps of the proposed processing pipeline are enumerated. Finally, the performance of the proposed framework is discussed.

Keywords Photo-mosaicing · Blending techniques

In this book a full approach for large-scale underwater image mosaicing and blending has been proposed. The presented pipeline extends the common photo-mosaicing techniques to the more complex and challenging underwater medium. The aim is the generation of giga-photo-mosaics over large areas (in the km^2 range), allowing the broad scale monitoring of seafloor extensions for geological, biological and environmental purposes, among others.

Deep-ocean imaging suffers from specific problems that require the application of specific solutions. The contributions of this book concern all the photo-mosaicing steps (image preprocessing, enhancing and blending) that can significantly improve the final image quality and visual pleasantness. Nevertheless, and without loss of generality, this pipeline can also be applied to the generation of terrestrial or aerial image panoramas.

Image blending is conceived as a set of stages that can be inserted into a 2D mosaicing pipeline in order to improve and enhance the quality of the final photo-mosaic. In Chap. 2, the common steps of image mosaicing were described, focusing on the particularities of their application in the underwater medium. Therefore, the use of navigation data and a topology estimation method as key steps in the registration process were also described. Furthermore, the proposed non-uniform illumination compensation strategy can also be used as a preprocessing step, allowing improvement of the quality in pair-wise image registration.

R. Prados et al., *Image Blending Techniques and their Application in Underwater Mosaicing*, SpringerBriefs in Computer Science, DOI: 10.1007/978-3-319-05558-9_6,
© The Author(s) 2014

A comprehensive state of the art in image blending techniques in 2D has been presented in Chap. 3. The most relevant methods intended to deal with aerial and satellite mapping, conventional terrestrial landscape panoramas and underwater imagery have been described, pointing out their strengths and weaknesses concerning their application in underwater photo-mosaicing. There are three main groups of blending methods in the literature. On the one hand, transition smoothing methods rely on fading the transition between neighboring images by appropriately fusing the overlapping pixel information around an arbitrarily selected seam. On the other hand, optimal seam finding methods are intended to find an optimally placed seam that minimizes the photometric or gradient differences between neighboring pixels around its path. Hybrid methods combine the benefits of both approaches by smoothing the transition along an optimally placed seam, and become the most adequate strategy to perform image blending in 2D, specially when dealing with images acquired in the underwater medium.

This book contributes to the state-of-art in large area image mosaicing methods for underwater surveys, focusing on the visual consistency and the detail enhancement of the generated photo-mosaics. The proposed framework, presented in Chap. 4, includes several steps that are inserted into the 2D mosaicing pipeline. In the pre-processing stage, a *depth dependent illumination compensation function* is computed and applied to the original images in order to solve the non-uniform illumination appearance due to light attenuation. This strategy uses a varying illumination compensation function based on a spatial sliding window, ensuring an appropriate compensation for images acquired at significantly different depths. Additionally, if precise depth information is not available, an *altitude estimation* based on the projection image size (once registered) has been proposed to be used at different steps in the pipeline. Concerning image enhancement, the contrast variability due to different acquisition altitudes has been compensated using an *adaptive contrast enhancement*, based on an image quality reference selected through a Total Variation (TV) criterion. This criterion has also been applied to prioritize the information coming from the *higher quality images* when building the first and second closest maps, which allows us to perform the graph cut on the overlapping regions. Consequently, the contribution from sharper and more visually pleasant images is higher than from contrastless or poorly detailed ones. In the blending step, the proposed graph-cut strategy operates in both the *image intensity domain* and the *image gradient domain* over the overlapping regions, in contrast with several state-of-the-art [1–3] methods working only in the intensity domain image differences. This approach allows finding an adequate seam even if the overlapping images have been acquired with different exposures. For a given image region acquired with two different exposures, an intensity domain approach will find photometric differences between pixels that do not correspond to real scene structure misalignments. A gradient domain method is unaffected by this problem since gradient values are not exposure dependent. The smooth transition around the optimally selected seam is performed in a *narrow strip*, ensuring the maximum sharpness possible and avoiding double contouring in that region. This smoothing is also performed in the gradient domain, as it also compensates for the possible different exposures between images. Finally, an out-of-core *blending strategy for very large-scale photo-mosaics*, i.e. Giga-photo-mosaics, has been developed and tested with real data, generating images in excess of 5 GPixel, and having, as the only limitation, the maximum size of the tile that can be processed in a given amount of RAM.

The approach proposed has been tested in several image sequences in Chap. 5, each one showing several specific underwater imagery problems. The large number of images in the sequences and their size lead to high dimension photo-mosaics, i.e. Giga-photo-mosaics. This fact has allowed the testing of the effectiveness of the out-of-core processing strategy proposed. Furthermore, the results obtained by the approach presented have been compared in selected areas with the results obtained by some of the most representative state-of-the-art blending methods. Our method has demonstrated to be as good as, or better than, the state-of-the-art techniques, outperforming them in many cases.

In the case of the Lucky Strike datasets, full scientific interpretation has been carried out [4, 5]. The benefits of using blended gigamosaics for interpretation tasks has been demonstrated in some examples. This imagery provides a view of the evolution of the hydrothermal system over long geological periods of time, and can thus be exploited to provide a comprehensive view of the different kinds of hydrothermal outflow in the Lucky Strike area, their distribution, and their relative abundances [4, 5], which was not available prior to obtaining these mosaics. In the case of the shipwreck survey, the photomosaic was the basis for planning archeological activities subsequently.

References

1. Kwatra, V., Schodl, A., Essa, I., Turk, G., Bobick, A.: Graphcut textures: image and video synthesis using graph cuts. ACM Trans. Graph (SIGGRAPH) **22**(3), 277–286 (2003)
2. Gracias, N., Mahoor, M., Negahdaripour, S.: Fast image blending using watersheds and graph cuts. Image Vis. Comput. **27**, 597–607 (2009)
3. Xiong, Y., Pulli, K.: Color correction based image blending for creating high resolution panoramic images on mobile devices. In: ACM SIGGRAPH Asia: Poster, SIGGRAPH Asia '09, NY, USA, New York (2009)
4. Barreyre, T., Escartin, J., Garcia, R., Cannat, M., Mittelstaedt, E., Prados, R.: Structure, temporal evolution, and heat flux estimates from a deep-sea hydrothermal field derived from seafloor image mosaics. Geochem. Geophys. Geosyst. **13**(4), 1–29 (2012)
5. Mittelstaedt, E., Escartin, J., Gracias, N., Olive, J.-A., Barreyre, T., Davaille, A., Cannat, M., Garcia, R.: Quantifying diffuse and discrete venting at the Tour Eiffel vent site, lucky strike hydrothermal field. Geochem. Geophys. Geosyst **13**(4), 1–18 (2012). ISSN: 1525-2027. doi:10.1029/2011GC003991